What the experts are saying about
How to Increase Your Website Traffic

This book delivers a series of powerful, practical principles to drive more traffic to your website and sell more than ever before.

—Brian Tracy
Author, *The Psychology of Selling*

Finally a book that shows you how to send more traffic to your website and convert that traffic to sales!

—T. Harv Eker
Author of the #1 *New York Times* Bestseller
Secrets of the Millionaire Mind

I'm a big fan of simplicity for success, and Khoa's new book lays out an easy-to-follow plan to increase your website traffic and convert those visitors to cash.

—Ali Brown
CEO & Founder, Ali International

Your website is invisible, unknown and relatively useless—unless people go there and do something. But how do you accomplish that? You read Khoa Bui's brilliant *How to Increase Your Website Traffic*, then follow his ultra-practical advice. Every single day, millions of people go online but don't visit your site. Khoa Bui wants to change that— and he can with his remarkable book. So he did his part. Now it's time for you to do yours. I predict success if you do.

—Jay Conrad Levinson
Father of Guerrilla Marketing
Author, *Guerrilla Marketing* series

How to Increase Your Website Traffic is a content-rich book, packed with powerful ideas that will help Internet entrepreneurs increase their sales and business profits. It is well written and the ideas are useful and practical. A great read for anyone who is serious about building an income stream online.

—Adam Khoo, Asia's #1 Success Coach
Author, *Secrets of Self-Made Millionaires*

I predict that businesses all over the world will soon be familiar with most of the concepts outlined in this book. Sales and marketing people everywhere will soon be talking about the very commonsense principles in *How To Increase Your Website Traffic* and how best to put these principles to work for their own businesses. If you want to know how to compete in the interactive universe of World Wide Web sites, then read this book. If you want to avoid the e-commerce trap of commoditization and margin pressure, then read this book. If you want just to better understand the kinds of marketing relationships that are most likely to develop in the age of interactivity, then read this book. This book is easy to read, concise, and to the point. Khoa Bui is the ultimate entrepreneur for the information age.

—Merry Riana
Bestselling Author of *A Gift from a Friend*

What a breath of fresh air to have an Internet book that is easy to read and packed with easy-to-implement, practical tools for business owners of any size business! Khoa Bui delivers a wealth of experience in *How to Increase Your Website Traffic*'s well-written, clear chapters. I was able to make changes to the way I have been doing business online immediately. This is a must-read for everyone who has anything at all to do with an online business.

—Judeth Wilson, Author, Speaker,
Entrepreneur, Business Owner of
Upfront Communications
Founder of *The Trainers Ultimate Toolkit*

How to Increase Your Website Traffic

Khoa Bui
www.khoa-bui.com

Entrepreneur. Press

Publisher: Jere Calmes
Cover Design: Andrew Welyczko, CWL Publishing Enterprises, Inc.
Editorial and Production Services: CWL Publishing Enterprises, Inc.,
Madison, Wisconsin, www.cwlpub.com

This publication is designed to provide accurate and authoritative information
in regard to the subject matter covered. It is sold with the understanding that
the publisher is not engaged in rendering legal, accounting, or other professional services. If legal advice or other expert assistance is required, the services
of a competent professional person should be sought.

> —From a Declaration of Principles jointly adopted by a
> Committee of the American Bar Association and
> a Committee of Publishers and Associations

ISBN   13: 978-1-59918-399-2
       10: 1-59918-399-4

Every effort has been made to ensure that the information in this book is
accurate and current at the time of publication. However, laws, regulations,
policies, contact information, and so on may be changed without notice.
This book is not a substitute for individual advice rendered by a professional
who is able to work with you one-on-one.

This book is dedicated to my loving family for giving me life

My mum, my dad, and my brother, Loan, Doi, and Luan,
"Without risk, I would have no life ..."

My loving partner, Hannah
"Without support, there would be no journey ..."

Contents

Preface

The reason I wrote this book was not for monetary gain or prestige, but simply because there were so many coincidences and events that "instructed me" that it was time to publish the results of my journey so that more people could benefit from them.

I've always enjoyed writing down my ideas. I still have my old journal from primary school and it's amazing to read how things were different back then. Years before the publication of this book, I managed to keep thousands of pages of notes on life, lessons learned, business, and so forth. There are times when I would wake up at 3 a.m. with ideas, grab a pen and paper, and write in the dark.

What really triggered me to write this book was the string of coincidences that occurred before its development. One of the things that happened was that I had an idea for a short book about some of the lessons I'd learned, and how they've helped me. Every night, I banged away at my keyboard on that topic, putting together great information, imagining how readers would benefit from it. But then I stopped that project and never returned.

One day I walked into the local bookstore and found the exact book title that I had been writing about. It was sitting in the "top 10 bestsellers" category. I guess that was the universe's way of telling me that I have something valuable to offer to the world and I shouldn't waste the opportunity again.

Another signal was that I continually received recommendations from my clients who felt I had a lot of great information to share. They would say that my ideas were useful, and that I should teach and write about them.

I also saw many positive results from my clients. Their websites were being positioned on the front page by search engines, and received more traffic, in addition to making thousands of dollars.

Great books about personal development, success, and business, and the great authors who wrote them also inspired me.

All of these coincidences added up, pushing my sense that it was finally time to put everything together, begin my journey, and give my knowledge and experience back to world.

This is my first book on increasing website traffic and it all started on my laptop with a chai tea latte in a local coffee shop. It finally ended in a different country 3,000 miles away. Over the duration of the project I wrote at 10,000 kilometers, flying high above the Asia Pacific, in airports waiting for delayed flights, at home, in my office, in cafés overlooking beautiful rivers, and in hotel rooms and apartments all over the world.

I wrote in poor countries and rich countries. Some parts were typed and others were recorded using voice dictation software. There were also days when I wrote for only five minutes and others when I wrote from sunup to sundown.

As I'm writing this and looking out the window from my new apartment I see cities stretching to the horizon, millions of people commuting to their jobs, and many boats traveling the rivers. This vista has made me realize how the strategies in this book have helped me get where I am today.

I hope this collection of my experiences, stories, and strategies helps you achieve greater success with your website.

They say it's easy to write a book but hard to complete it. I agree with that statement. Anyone can type at a keyboard but having the discipline to do it every day and transform ideas into a book is a different story. There were many times when I felt this project was a bad idea and others when it seemed like I was on the right track. Either way, what really kept me going were the "messages" I received that pushed me to get it done.

This book is divided into five parts. The first part is the story of my journey online. The second part covers the mandatory, fundamental "Cash Website Triangle." You must first understand this before proceeding with your online ventures. The third part covers a wealth of paid, free, online, and offline traffic generation strategies. The fourth part of the book covers marketing and how to convert your traffic into sales. Each chapter also comes with a list of Quick Action Steps for you to take away and apply. The final part of the book briefly covers your product or service.

My goal is to provide you with as much valuable information as possible to help you get better results from your website. There are many poorly designed and managed websites out there. I hope this book acts as a guide to unearth life success for you, whether it's financial or lifestyle.

I focused on the core fundamentals of traffic generation and marketing that will assist you many years to come, even as technology advances. There are new technological advances in website function every year but the core fundamentals will never change.

I hope you find this book easy to read, digest, and apply, but what I hope the most is that the lessons in it help you as much as they've helped me.

Acknowledgments

If I have seen further, it is by standing on the shoulders of giants.

—Issac Newton

I would not be where I am today without the following mentors. I would like to sincerely thank Jim Rohn for his wisdom over the years; you will always be remembered by the millions of people you've helped.

Brian Tracy, thank you for all your valuable knowledge and humble advice. Your teachings have helped me in so many ways. Tony Robbins, thank you for helping me begin the journey of self-development and keep the momentum flowing. Steven Covey, thank you for helping me maintain a healthy perspective on life. Adam Khoo, thank you for giving me the inspiration and clarity in business. Og Mandino, I thank for his fantastic story of survival and homelessness to becoming one of the most successful people in the world. I would also like to thank the publishing team at Entrepreneur Press. You have made my dream possible. Thank you. There are many more people who have helped me but you already know who you are.

I would also like to acknowledge all the entrepreneurs who are the true warriors of the planet. They go into battle every single day with great courage, get punched, kicked, rejected, and at the end of it all, still crawl forward, get back up, and change history. From the struggling single mothers to the top entrepreneurs of the world, you are my inspiration. You are the movers and shakers of the world.

Finally, as much as I hate to admit this, I would also like to thank the difficulties in my past, present, and future. I've come to accept that we will always meet face-to-face, and it would be hard to imagine how far I would go if you were not there to make me stronger and push me beyond my comfort zone. You are my enemies, but at the same time disguised as my friends. Thank you.

Confessions of
an Entrepreneur

One night I was driving my car down a long, dark, and dangerous road. It was an old beat-up car I'd purchased with all my savings. Its list of problems was long and included an engine that continually overheated, almost-bald tires, and broken windshield wipers. It was raining heavily that night and my damaged wipers were not helping me see ahead.

The road was slippery and I had to continually slow down to make sure I wouldn't slip off and smash into a pole. A glance at my engine gauge showed that it was nearly in the red zone but I reassured myself that I wasn't very far from home. There were times when I had to park the car by the side of the road and wait for a whole hour for it to cool but I guess I was lucky that night and didn't need to do that.

I managed to keep the engine temperature just out of the red zone by not accelerating too much uphill and whenever I made it up the hill I would just let the car coast to minimize engine use. I also had other ways of keeping it cool, like keeping the air conditioner turned off.

As my car rolled, the only thing I could see were red traffic lights and headlights passing through the busy intersection at the bottom of the hill. At that point, I began thinking about where my life was. I realized that I'd spent over 10 years in school and another six years in university. During that time, I'd toiled over countless exams, research, assignments, and homework. I used to study long into the night with the dream of landing a good IT job or owning a business in that industry.

All my friends had gotten jobs right after they finished university. I seemed to be the only one who struggled and companies didn't want to hire. Finally, after 11 months of cover letters, résumé rewrites, job applications, and interviews, I got lucky and landed a job as a software developer.

After two and a half years, I realized that a software programming job was not right for me. It was time to chase my dream and start my own web design business. I thought about the fact that as a result of 16 years of schooling, two years of employment and two years of running that business, I was driving an old, beat-up car with broken wipers, bald tires, and an overheating engine.

Not only was my car was struggling but my business was struggling, as well. I became frustrated with my business problems. I couldn't get any clients, generate any website traffic, or make any online sales. My website was even banned from search engines and I received negative feedback from one person commenting, "Your website looks like ∗∗∗∗ and you're supposed to be a web design company!"

Finally, the scariest fact was that I only made $200 in two years of running my business! It was certainly not enough to fund my dreams and lifestyle. It was at that moment that I faced reality and realized that I was a failure.

I felt like a loser who had wasted his entire life working toward something that never succeeded. It was the feeling of preparing my whole life for something, being given a chance, and then missing my opportunity. I started to imagine how athletes feel when they spend their whole lives training, waking up early in the morning to practice over and over. Finally when it's time to compete in the world, they miss their goal by a millisecond or a centimeter, and then it's over. That's how I felt, like it was over.

As I got closer to the traffic lights, cars were still crossing through the intersection and I didn't even bother to hit the brakes. I just let my car roll faster toward the swarm of cars so I could end it right there and start over again. I was hoping for a crash. There are dark moments in your life when you feel like giving up and forget everyone else around you. That night was my dark moment.

Then all of a sudden, it hit me like a car crash. Fortunately, it wasn't a car crash. It was an epiphany.

The Epiphany

The epiphany was that I was doing the wrong things in my business. I was reading the wrong books, and spending time on the wrong aspects of the business. I'd been spending months writing a business plan, designing beautiful business cards and logos, and preparing my legal structure. Many people had given me advice about what to do to be successful, but I wasn't achieving any sort of success at all.

I also spent a lot of money on the wrong books, research, and advertising material, which generated zero income for me. Many of the books I bought talked about how to go from zero to millionaire in record time. But let's be honest here, did I really believe I could do that?

I knew I had to make a decision about what I was going to do next because time was running out.

The Life-Changing Decision

It was then I realized I'd made a lot of mistakes and needed to wipe the slate clean and start again, without purposely injuring myself or someone else. I decided to start another company the next morning. This time, I wasn't going to spend time or money on business plans, reports, invoices, or other tedious activities. This time, I was going to focus my efforts on generating sales and tweak my business later.

That's it!

I didn't care if I didn't have a business plan or the right infrastructure or perfect clothes and shoes for client meetings. I didn't bother with stationery or fridge magnets anymore. None of those things bought me any business. Two hundred dollars in two years was a good indicator that what I'd been doing wasn't working.

This time, I was going to get out there and actively find clients. That night, I hit the brakes and started my life over. My goal was to generate more business with my website.

Starting Over

A few months later, I made huge breakthroughs with my business and website. I attracted more clients than ever before, managed to find ways to attract massive traffic to my website, and even discovered how to convert that traffic into thousands of dollars in sales each month.

As a result, that income enabled me to buy my dream apartment next to a beautiful river, just minutes from the city. It also allowed me to travel the world and visit my dream destinations of Italy, France, Austria, Germany, Hong Kong, New York, Hawaii, and more. My ideas also led me to launch several other high-traffic websites that generated income while I slept.

I was also able to achieve another dream, which was to contribute thousands of dollars to charity instead of the smaller donations I used to give. I was only 26 years old and my dream had come true!

This book contains the techniques and strategies I used to turn my life around, from rolling my car down hill toward an accident to making thousands of dollars a month and flying around the world, visiting dream destinations.

It never ceases to amaze me how just a few minor tweaks to your website can massively increase your income online and dramatically change your life. The great news about this book is that I've written it in an easy-to-digest style so you can derive the same results that I did.

It's like riding a bike.

Think of the first time you rode your bike. You probably hopped on the seat and fell off immediately. You tried it again and fell off. Eventually, you managed to balance sitting on the seat. When you tried to pedal, you may have fallen off again or slowly started moving.

That's the purpose of my book.

There are many books out there that expect you ride in the Tour de France when you can't even balance on a bike. You have to learn how to crawl before you walk and eventually run.

Therefore, this book is not about getting you to make millions online; rather, it's about helping you crawl first in making your first thousand dollars online by driving more traffic to your site, and then converting that traffic to sales.

Once you've achieved your goal of generating that first thousand, all you have to do is duplicate what you did over and over until you hit your financial target.

If making that amount of money doesn't fuel your burning desire, then I suggest you to put this book down or give it to someone who may benefit from it.

However, if you're interested in learning how to make more money with your website that will give you a second income, help you save for your next overseas holiday, put together a deposit on a new home or purchase that car you've wanted (one that has window wipers that actually work), I invite you to keep reading.

Now, let's start the journey and get you sitting on that bike.

2

The Cash
Website Triangle

What I'm about to show you is a result of over 15 years of experimenting, testing, refining, spending money, and losing money. The result came from building over 100 websites from scratch. I've analyzed thousands of websites, which all seemed to follow a specific pattern.

All those late nights designing and building accumulated into something valuable that I'm about to share with you.

If I could show you a diagram of what I believe is the foundation of all website success, it would show that no matter how far into the future you reach, this diagram, or formula, will function positively in a capitalist society.

What if there were one foundation, principle, or path that would guarantee online success? What would it be?

I answered that question by constructing my Cash Website Triangle diagram.

This diagram is the only guide you need for online success. Many websites use the principles explained in this chapter. I've seen other people making vast amounts of money with their websites using them. Their tools and methods all vary but the principals are the same. As technology advances, this diagram will still stand true.

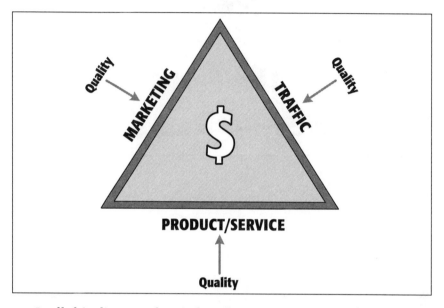

I call this diagram the Cash Website Triangle©.

How does this diagram work? I believe there are three factors that are necessary for a website to generate income. One can't exist without the others and they all depend on one another. Each side has pressure from the amount of quality being applied to it.

A triangle requires all three sides to be stable. If you were to remove one side, the triangle would collapse; therefore, each side depends on the others to maintain the structure.

The three sides are:

- Marketing
- Traffic
- Product/Service

In the next few sections, I give you an overview of each category but they won't be complete because there is so much information to cover, which would easily fill another book. We get into pertinent details later in the process.

The Marketing Side of the Triangle

Marketing is the way in which you present your information to the public so it can take action. For example, if you were marketing wheatgrass juice, you would want to make it attractive to a specific audience.

Your website could target health-conscious people by including content that touts the health attributes of your juice above all others. You may include data on nutritional content and the functions of those vitamins, minerals, and amino acids in preventing certain diseases, or you might provide quotes from medical health professionals on the benefits of drinking wheatgrass juice.

When you research your target market you'll want to investigate the reasons your target audience chooses certain brands of wheatgrass juice. Is it because of health, price, status, or convenience? Or does it taste more palatable?

What would happen if you matched targeted quality traffic (the right demographic on your site) and quality product (healthy, high-quality juice) with very poor marketing?

This is what would happen:

A health-conscious man wants to lose weight and his doctor advises him to increase his nutritional intake of vitamins, minerals, and amino acids through a sensible diet, daily vitamin supplements, and an exercise program. The man goes online to order a supplement and finds your juice, with all of the vitamins, minerals, and amino acids already in it.

He also finds that your product is grown organically in mineral-rich soil and harvested with a fair trade process, indicating that it is a quality product. When he tries to move forward in searching your site he sees a generic message such as:

"We are the premier wheatgrass distributors in the world. The quality of our product is guaranteed."

Notice anything familiar? The nonspecific copy makes it sound like every other health supplement peddler out there.

He clicks around some more and discovers snazzy photos of your delivery trucks and storage facility. He keeps searching because your site is cluttered and it's hard for him to find what he needs. Not only can he not find that specific mineral information, but each page takes a long time to load, indicating poor design; not exactly the image of a top-notch company, and possibly a shoddy product, as well.

He loses patience looking for the mineral attributes and leaves to go search for another company that will provide him with "getting healthy with vitamins and minerals."

You've just lost a customer (and possibly more, had he referred his friends, as well). The copy "getting healthy with vitamins and minerals" should have been on the front page of your website with easy navigation.

The quality of marketing on your site was poor and didn't match the needs of your customer. He was searching for something that was there, but you made it too hard for him to find it. You went to the trouble of getting the right traffic, but didn't support the triangle, and it collapsed.

Effective communication is as essential as attracting your target audience. Can you see how important the cash website triangle is?

Marketing is all about researching your target market and providing the right product to match with that market. It's also about presenting your website/information in a way that persuades other people to take action.

> *Marketing is all about researching your target market and providing the right product for it.*

Here's an example of the way your website could have captured a query or sale from that visitor:

A video begins to play on your homepage in which a healthy-looking person (or celebrity) talks about his newfound health. He might say something like "Years ago I was unfit and overweight, yet undernourished. My doctor warned that I was at high risk for cancer, diabetes, and heart disease. I was advised to adopt a diet high in antioxidants and start up a sensible exercise program. I found that drinking Bingo Wheatgrass Juice with high antioxidant content accomplishes my goals when I don't have time to eat home-prepared meals, by providing 20 times the amount found in vegetables, in one shot of juice. I stuck with my exercise program, ate a healthy diet, and drank Bingo Wheatgrass Juice daily, and passed my last medical exam with flying colors. I feel optimistic about the prospect of walking my daughter down the aisle and even becoming a grandparent! I highly recommend Bingo Wheatgrass Juice."

Your website should contain specific examples of the end result of using your product, not just promises of what it will do. You can never have enough concrete, before-and-after testimonials and photographs that viewers see as proof.

Use the lingo of your audience. If your target audience is teenagers, research current slang online and use that. If your audience is a polished, professional crowd, then use a sophisticated writing style or hire a copywriter. Instead of making general statements, get specific about how the attributes for your product will help your consumer, in easy-to-understand language.

Turn this: Bingo Wheatgrass Juice has higher amino acid and vitamin B12 content than other wheatgrass juices.

Into this: 15 pounds of Bingo Wheatgrass has the nutritional value of 350 pounds of ordinary garden vegetables. Pressed for time? You do the math! Drink a shot of Bingo and you've covered your vitamin requirements for the whole day.

Another example of turning product attributes into persuasive copy for your viewers is:

"Sometimes successful people living in the fast lane get hooked on coffee and the way it provides more energy for them. The problem is, you are borrowing energy from your body, like overdrawing a bank account. Eventually it will catch up with you, leaving you depleted.

"Getting in shape would provide you with more energy, as well as a highly nutritional diet. Drinking Bingo Wheatgrass Juice helps accomplish both of these goals at once, giving your body the energy it needs to achieve your fitness goals by providing an unsurpassed level of nutrition in a short time. Many of our clients have suddenly excelled in their fitness programs and lost that lingering weight just by adding Bingo to their regimen. If you don't feel improvement in your overall health in two weeks, we'll refund your money."

Imagine this information supported by photos of attractive, fit people engaged in high-energy activities like running, biking, or speaking to a group, alongside well-written testimonials.

Make sure that the colors you use are consistent with ones that match your target market's interests. An example could be researching what health-conscious people buy, where they go, what they eat. From there, you can see the which colors grab their attention. I know it may sound a bit strange but you'll be surprised how consistent and effective colors can be in getting your attention.

Those are just a few ways in which you can improve your marketing. Remember that the more time you spend on marketing, the more it will improve your website results.

The Traffic Side of the Triangle

Everyone wants more traffic flowing through their website. But the wrong kind of traffic isn't going to do anything for you, no matter how high the numbers are. If you have thousands of people perusing your site in search of "wheatgrass juicing machines" instead of "wheatgrass juice," they'll just keep on traveling out virtual the door.

Your only goals for getting traffic to your site should be those that attract your exact demographic. While the person who wants to buy a machine and juice their own wheatgrass at home may be similar to the person who wants to buy your juice, it's not exact. The person purchasing a machine probably has more time on their hands and may not be interested in paying for convenience the way the customer who wants a quick fix of nutrition would be.

That one slight difference could undermine everything.

> *Your website traffic must be that of a targeted audience. I cannot stress this enough and I'll say it again:* Your website traffic must be that of a targeted audience.

I know everyone wants more traffic on their website, however what everyone really should want is more targeted traffic. The reason why targeted traffic is more important than just traffic is that the targeted traffic group is people who are already interested in what you're offering.

It's much easier to sell your products and services on your website if people are genuinely interested in what you're offering. It's hard to sell a product to someone who doesn't have an interest in it; you'll be fighting an uphill battle. It's like giving out flyers promoting heaters in the middle of the desert.

By having targeted traffic, life will be easier for you.

Let's say you own a website that sells a range of beautiful wedding dresses and gets 100 visitors per day to it. However, those 100 visitors are only interested in purchasing dresses for their school prom. They would not be interested in your product because there was a slight difference in targeted traffic. One group wanted dresses for weddings and the other wanted dresses for their school prom. They were of different age groups and interests and had differing needs.

You may have achieved your goal of getting 100 visitors per day, but what you didn't achieve was your core goal of matching your product with the right target market.

More opportunities you could have taken advantage of while that traffic was flowing through your site include:

- Selling additional wedding dresses and other accessories
- Getting visitors to sign up for your report on "The Top 7 Mistakes Brides Make When Purchasing a Wedding Dress"

- Getting people to sign up for your newsletter
- Capturing their information to build up your database of leads to communicate with them later

Always focus on your goal when attracting targeted traffic to your website.

When I started my web design business, I really didn't have a clue what I was doing. I was learning by trial and error.

At one point, I wanted to try advertising because that's what everyone else was doing. I saw people using Google's PPC (pay per click) method and decided to do the same.

I structured my advertising so that whenever someone typed "web design" in Google, my website link would appear in the Google Ads section. To my surprise, I found that the rate for advertising with that one phrase was $5.70 per click. I thought that was expensive but that I'd give it a shot anyway because everyone else was doing it.

Here's what happened: I wanted to get 100 visitors on my website, so I set up the ad and began advertising. Almost immediately I started getting more traffic. It was great. Right away someone clicked on the link, then a few minutes later, someone else, and so on.

While I was watching people click on my ad, I couldn't help noticing that my cost was adding up really fast. I still wasn't getting any inquiries. Eventually, I stopped the advertising and looked at my results.

I paid a couple hundred dollars within a few minutes but didn't get one query. No business or clients.

A few months later, I realized that the advertising failure wasn't Google's fault, it was mine for not understanding how it worked.

My conclusion was that Internet surfers typing "web design" in the Google search box casts a wide net. Those people could have been searching for any number of things related or unrelated to my product, such as:

- Careers in web design
- The history of web design
- Examples of web design
- How to be a web designer
- Web designers
- Web design companies
- Freelance web design
- Web design tools

The list goes on.

Let's say that out of the 100 people who clicked on my advertisement, 99 of them were searching for something else and only one was actually looking for a web design company.

When that one person interested in a web design company found my website they probably glanced around and left because they quickly lost interest. Here are some possible reasons why:

- They didn't like the look and feel of my website.
- They wanted to work with someone in their geographic area.
- They didn't connect with content on my website.
- They assumed that it was either too expensive or too cheap.
- They didn't like the work I displayed.
- They were after something other than web design.

After looking at that result, I wondered about the possibility of attracting 100 people who were actually interested in a web design company in my hometown of Perth. Wouldn't that increase my odds?

About seven months later, I reengineered my advertising to focus on a targeted audience. From just that change I made $30,000 without advertising and some minor tweaking. It was a huge step from making only a couple hundred dollars to making thousands. The funny part was that I didn't direct much traffic to my website but was able to easily convert the little targeted traffic I did into customers.

I had started discovering the secrets of the cash website triangle.

> *The secret of the Cash Website Triangle is that targeted, quality traffic, plus targeted, quality marketing, plus targeted, quality products or service equals customers.*

The Products and Services Side of the Triangle

This is the point in the process where a lot of people start working on the product or service that makes up their business.

Although having great products and services are important, they aren't an absolute necessity for you to succeed online. There are lots of great ideas out there for wonderful products and services that will never make it due to poor marketing.

> *There are many great products out there that fail to sell because of poor marketing.*

You can see now that there are other factors to learn about to make your website a success. Let me tell you a story.

When I first started my web design business I was working for a rapidly growing software development company in the education sector with about 40 employees.

My role as a software developer was to provide programming support to the other developers. There were six developers on my team and we all contributed to one product.

We programmed our software using software languages like ASP.NET, Javascript, PHP, and SQL.

During my time there, I realized that no matter what happened, I would always need to keep my skills up to date because the programming languages we used updated their versions each year. ASP.NET 1.0 would be upgraded to ASP.NET 2.0, which we would have to learn and apply to our work.

I didn't like it.

As soon as I realized that I would need to upgrade my programming skills every year, the future didn't look so bright. I would have to keep learning new language versions each year just to keep myself employed and even that didn't guarantee job security because a lot of companies were outsourcing jobs like mine overseas.

I was being paid around $24 an hour and outsourced projects were only being billed at around $10 an hour. I could see that I was setting myself up to be vulnerable. Not only was I investing a lot of time and energy into programming software, but I would also always be a programmer, competing with better, cheaper programmers who charged half as much and worked twice as hard.

That thought alone didn't sit very well with me. It was then that I decided to quit and create my own software development company that I could work at part time.

When I first started my first software development company, a friend who owned a limousine company wanted software to handle his bookings and reservations. I jumped at the opportunity to design it for him.

I spent nearly every waking hour building and programming the software and refining the code, making the product fantastic, and making sure it worked well. I didn't see much of my friends as I worked late into the night, dreaming of seeing my software being used by his company.

I spent nearly six months working on it. Finally, I showed the demo to the client and he was happy with the end result and how it worked.

He later said that because it was a small program he was only willing to pay $300–$500 for it. I knew it was worth much more than that but didn't care because it was a great product. I was really proud of my efforts, especially the way I coded it.

When I researched other popular reservation software I discovered something really amazing. They were charging $3,000–$10,000 for their product, and it didn't even have the number of features mine did.

I was so frustrated!

How come they were able to charge so much when my software was worth so much more? Then it dawned on me that the companies that were able to get a lot of money for their products were actually marketers rather than product developers.

There was something in addition to programming that I needed to learn to raise more capital. It was marketing and selling.

> *Building a great product is only part of the equation. You must learn how to market and sell it.*

I'm not suggesting that you stop focusing on your product but many people believe that simply focusing their efforts on the best product will be enough to succeed.

There are countless products and ideas that are created but never discovered by an audience. Giant companies spend millions on advertising and marketing because those tools are needed to build awareness of their products.

Offering your product or service to the marketplace is not only financially rewarding but also emotionally fulfilling.

Seeing your creation out there being used by others is a satisfying feeling. Therefore I won't focus too much on building a great product because I know that if you're reading this book, you're probably genuinely interested in building your business and really do contribute great products and services to the marketplace.

In summary, let's say that you have great marketing and targeted traffic and you've achieved your goal of getting people to purchase your product. Let's suppose, though, that your product lacks quality, is broken, or doesn't deliver what you promise.

If that's the case, your phone will be tied up with angry customers demanding refunds. You'll lose sales and build a bad reputation at the same time. Also, no one likes negative feedback on something they've spent many years creating. All of this adds up to the fact that although you've got great marketing and traffic, your low-quality product will cause the triangle to collapse.

It's vital to have all three sides of the cash website triangle working effectively. You need the three facets of quality traffic, quality marketing, and a quality product operating at full force, at the same time.

If you can accomplish that, you'll position yourself for website success.

The Hidden Bonus

Even though this book largely focuses on traffic generation, it also covers marketing. The product and service side of the triangle rests solely on you.

The goal of this book is not just to help you send more traffic to your website but to also help you convert that traffic to sales. Once you start to generate income by applying my principles, you'll enjoy the benefits of living the lifestyle you want.

Quick Action Steps

Write down who your target audience is. Make sure it's *descriptive* and *specific* rather than general. For example, my target audience is business owners in the health industry who earn over $500,000 annually and have five or more employees between 40 and 60 years of age. The more detail, the better.

3

The Cash Website Triangle: The Traffic Side

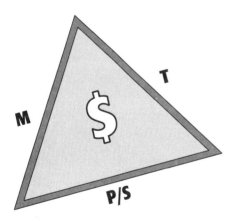

This section of the book covers various traffic generation strategies I've successfully used over the years. My book is based on actual strategies, not just theory. Most of the information is from a bird's eye view, but as you get closer to the ground you'll see the different areas in more detail.

As you read the technical aspects of this and other chapters, don't worry. I give you the basic ideas behind these materials and explain them as simply as possible.

So I encourage you to continue reading the book to the end. I don't expect you to become a coder, but to just learn the principles so you can work with and inform your web developer about what you want.

There are ideas in this book you may find obvious, but you'll be surprised that most people neglect these points and therefore fail to generate the results they want from their site. These principles of traffic generation are what I consider foundations.

New technology will emerge every year but these foundations won't change and you can always depend on them. You'll always need a large number of people moving through your site, a way to convert them into customers, and a product to offer them whether you use a website or not.

The Two Major Traffic Generation Models and How You Can Use Them to Your Advantage

There are two ways to generate traffic on your website. Most people think that if you stick with one strategy, you'll get the best results, but it really depends on your situation.

Each traffic generation method has its advantages and disadvantages; therefore, it's important to understand how each works. There are many strategies to attract traffic to your website but those fall into two categories:

1. Paid traffic
2. Free traffic

I explain this more using the Traffic Generation Matrix (see Table 3-1).

The Paid Traffic Model

With the Paid Traffic model, you get results almost immediately. This is an ideal solution if you have a product you need to launch within a certain time frame. It's ideal to test your product in the marketplace first to see if you receive a good response. If you do, you can always invest more money into paid traffic.

Paid traffic is a great way to test your product in the marketplace before you invest more capital.

	Free Traffic Model	Paid Traffic Model
Examples	• Blogs • Article marketing • Social networking • Press releases • Article directories • YouTube • Joint ventures	• Google Adwords • Newspaper advertising • Radio advertising • Signage • Banners • TV advertising • Search engine optimization (SEO)
Advantages	• You don't to continually spend money to get traffic. • Traffic will be sent to you forever. • Your traffic will tend to increase over time. • Work really hard once and the rest is on autopilot. • You build a good relationship with your customers first. • You're given a lot of room for testing in the long run.	• You receive instant traffic on your website. • You'll receive a huge, explosive surge of traffic. • Your traffic is mostly targeted. • You can immediately test your products in the marketplace and see the results.
Disadvantages	• Requires a lot of upfront investment of your energy. • Requires a lot of your time to build the traffic components. • Your traffic tends to be general instead of targeted. • The results generated will take a lot longer for you to receive.	• Can be expensive to continually send traffic to your website. • You can lose a lot of money if you don't advertise in the right medium. • To make money, you need to know your numbers and whether advertising in that particular medium will pay for itself.

Table 3-1. The Traffic Generation Matrix

One effective way to get paid traffic to your site is through Google Adwords. There are many other search engines that offer the same service, but at the moment Google Adwords is the most popular way to get paid traffic to your site.

With Google Adwords, you place an ad on search engines and if your ad is written effectively you receive clicks on your website link. Each click on your website link costs you money. Depending on your market, whether it's competitive or not, it ranges between $0.10 a click to $10 a click or even more.

One of the most important things about using paid traffic is that you obviously need to do your homework before you advertise. If you don't make any calculations, you're seriously risking your advertising dollars. Here's an example:

Let's say you sell business widgets for $5. You place a $1,000 ad in a newspaper with a readership of 200,000. How many sales do you have to make to pay for the ad?

You need 200 customers to pay for your advertisement. You should also make a net profit so that number will even be greater. Let's say your business widget now costs $100. How many sales do you now have to make to pay off your advertisement? Only 10.

So now the question is, in which is scenario is easier to make money? Finding 200+ customers or only 10?

There are additional variables you need to take into consideration. Is the newspaper a suitable advertising medium to reach your target market of business executives? If everyone reading the newspaper were an employee, would your message be effective in selling business widgets? Of course not. You would have spent $1,000 for nothing.

Another variable you need to test when it comes to paid traffic advertising is your conversion rate.

Let's say that you've never written an effective ad before and decide to advertise in the newspaper. Your ad pulls in only one call. Out of 200,000 people who might have seen your ad, one person called, which means that your ad has a conversion rate of 0.000005 percent. Let's say you knew how to write effective ads that make the phone ring and your conversion rate was 10 percent. That means that 10 percent of 200,000 people equals $20,000 in sales; $20,000 in sales multiplied by 100 business widgets equals $2 million dollars!

The reality is that standard ads only pull between 1 and 3 percent, and it's best to work your numbers first so you can win with the worst-case scenario. You also have to make sure your market matches your target customer. There's no point in advertising fresh pumpkins in a dog-training magazine.

The reality is, you must know how to convert the traffic on your website to sales. Knowing how to increase your conversion rate is an art form. Countless books have been written on the subject and many people are known to have a conversion rate of 70 percent and higher. Therefore, this topic is huge, and I can't possibly write all about it in this book; however, I do give you a few tactics to help increase your conversion rate.

> *The reality is, you must know how to convert the traffic on your website into sales.*

How do I know all of this? I've lost thousands of my own dollars over the years from using paid traffic advertising without first doing the proper research. I remember placing an ad in the paper for which I paid $800. I waited by the phone when the paper came out. My calculations predicted that even in the worst-case scenario, I would receive 100 calls that day. I was so confident the phone would ring that I had my pen and pad ready to accept orders.

At the end of the day, my end results were:

- Seven online queries
- Three phone calls
- One snail mail response

Even though I received responses, I felt devastated because I was supposed to receive many more. I later thought about why it didn't work out the way I planned. I determined the reason was that my target market was wrong. The newspaper I advertised in mainly served people who weren't starting businesses and didn't need my services.

That was the price I paid for being lazy. Researching your advertising medium really doesn't take that much time. All it takes is a nice cup of coffee and an hour or two. Always do your research first.

Being lazy costs money.

One of the best things about paid traffic is that you can get results immediately to test and measure your progress. If you're testing a new product and want people to participate immediately, you should pay for an ad that'll bring targeted traffic to you. Instead of waiting for weeks for people to check out your product, you can get results straightaway. It will save you lots of time. Paid traffic is a great strategy for research and lead generation.

Here are some ideal ways to use it:

- Create a survey site to research your specific market
- Build a database of prospects so you can build a business relationship with them
- Send highly targeted traffic to your website

One of the most popular ways to use paid traffic is to build your database. By building your database of prospects, you're building a massive database that you can continuously talk directly to and inform of any special promotions or events.

Let's say you spend money on paid traffic to simply get people to sign up for a free service. You build a database of 2,000 people, complete with names and e-mail addresses. Over time, you build a relationship with your database and send out a promotion for your services, selling them for $197. If only 1 percent of 2,000 people responds to your promotion, that's 20 customers. Twenty customers multiplied by $197 equals $3,940.

Let's put it another way. Let's say you took that $3,940, drove to your nearest airport and booked a round trip flight to Hawaii. It's Friday night and you fly to Hawaii. You spend the next few days sitting on the beach, drinking margaritas, watching the sun set, walking around, and having fun. On Monday, you return to your office and start work again.

What just happened? By learning how to effectively use paid traffic advertising, you were able to afford a quick vacation. Isn't that nice? Let me remind you that you're not just doing this for the money. You're doing this for a higher purpose. Yes, that's drinking margaritas on the beach.

The Free Traffic Model

One of the most unfortunate things about human nature is that most of us tend to look for shortcuts. If we want to lose weight, we try to do it without spending any energy; we would rather take a pill and lose weight instead of going for a run and eating healthy foods.

The same goes with generating free traffic. Many people would like to get traffic on their website for free but don't want to spend the time and energy to get it.

One of the major advantages of free traffic is that you get long-term results but most importantly, don't need to pay for them. Free traffic is extremely profitable and a strong strategy in getting repeat customer sales with your website. However, it does require some effort and patience before you'll see results.

One of the most powerful ways to generate traffic on your website is to write content. Writing content is the cornerstone of getting free traffic. If you continually write effective articles rich in content and keywords, then you're on your way to attracting traffic to your website without paying for it. A common way to get free traffic is to create a blog site, which I explain to you in a later chapter.

One of the most powerful ways to generate free traffic is to write quality content.

In the long term, if you focus your efforts on attracting free traffic, you'll have a better chance of profiting. Unlike paid traffic, there are no advertising expenses so your profit is larger.

The calculations are the same as with paid traffic. If you generate enough traffic to your site, a percentage of that traffic converts to sales. But you have to wait for it.

There are many people who love to write and are currently receiving millions of visitors each day on their website for those efforts, which they've invested several months or even years in. The reason that works is because they are in a hungry market with a lot of visitors searching for that specific information and the website owners are dedicated to writing every day about their passions.

If you think this sounds like you, then free traffic generation is a good path for you.

Many people usually start off with a small budget to fund their business ventures so free traffic generation is their most obvious means to get customers.

Here's a step-by-step way to get free traffic to your website and convert that traffic to sales.

My Step-by-Step System for Building Free Traffic and Converting That Traffic to Sales

1. Research your market online to uncover the preferences of your target readers.
2. If that market is hungry for content and you're passionate about the topic that they crave, create a blog site targeting a subniche in that category.
3. Write a keyword-rich article every day on that niche.
4. Keep writing.
5. Keep writing.
6. See your results.
7. Keep writing.
8. Generate sales.
9. Keep writing.
10. Generate sales.
11. Keep writing.

I know someone who was really passionate about personal development. He read countless books on it. One day he decided to transform his passion to writing about all his thoughts on that field.

Because he was passionate about that subject matter, he was always writing original content and focused on helping people. When he started, he barely attracted any traffic to his website but didn't care. He kept writing.

Nine months later, he noticed that his website received an exponential spike in traffic. All the articles he wrote were being linked to people all over the world who were writing about him and his original content. Today he receives millions of visitors each month and monetizes that traffic by placing ads on his blog.

His website has made him financially free and his efforts turned to profits and paid for his house and lifestyle. All of this occurred because he was passionate about what he was doing and was in an appropriately matched, hungry market.

> *If you're passionate about a popular industry and work every day to create quality content about it, your chance of success rises significantly.*

Of course, most people want the end result of this kind of success but don't want to invest the time and energy required to achieve it.

Therefore you must decide which traffic generation model is right for your situation.

Quick Action Steps

1. Looking at the traffic generation matrix early in this chapter, which model do you feel suits your current situation? Free, paid, or both?
2. Based on your answers to question 1, pick one strategy and aim to spend one hour focusing on it this month. You can research, study, and apply it. Just allocate one hour of your time to work on one method.
3. Create a basic marketing campaign spreadsheet that contains the following information:
   a. How many targeted visitors will you get by advertising through media like newspaper, websites, and radio?

b. How much does your product or service cost?

c. How much does its ad cost?

d. How many sales do you need to make to pay for the ad?

e. Work out the margins for your product. If you have a product selling for $100 and it takes $80 to produce it, including expenses, your margin will be 80 percent.

f. Work out your worst-case scenario. If only 1 percent of the total targeted readers took action because of your ad, would you still be able to pay for it and make a profit?

Finally, when you look over the numbers, what would you change to get better results? Would you change the price of your product, the number of targeted visitors to your ad, or your margins?

4

How to Attract Free Traffic to Your Website Using These Three Traffic-Generation Strategies

One of my favorite movies is *Field of Dreams*. Kevin Costner is out in his cornfield and begins hearing mysterious voices. One day, he hears a gentle voice whisper, "If you build it, they will come." Costner's character takes action and eventually builds a baseball field in the middle of his corn farm, which satisfies one of his long-lost and repressed dreams.

The Online Field of Dreams

So, what does this have to do with getting more traffic to your website? The answer is this: Many people believe that once you build a website you'll automatically be swamped with traffic and customers beating a path to your door. Unfortunately, this won't happen unless you market your website well.

> *In the online world, I would say that if you build it, they won't come unless you frequently market it.*

One of the biggest secrets behind generating more sales and free traffic is to use proper online sources. If you want to see your website climb the search engines, an increase in traffic, and more queries, follow the steps I enumerate, and guess what? The techniques cost you nothing.

The Three Most Powerful Online Marketing Strategies

If you want to get an explosion of traffic on your website and increase your sales and queries, then let me introduce the three most powerful online marketing methods you can apply to your website right now and it won't cost you a cent. Here they are:

Secret Weapon Online Strategy #1: Recording Compelling Videos

Videos are not just a great traffic-generation tool but they are also a wonderful way for people to get to know and build a level of trust with you. They aren't as difficult as you may think to set up on your website.

> *Video builds trust.*

Here are five steps to quickly creating your first video without spending a cent:

1. If you have a digital camera, simply turn the video on.
2. Begin recording a quick overview of your topic.
3. Plug the camera into your computer.
4. Download the file to your computer.
5. Upload that video to popular video sites.

There are free video websites out there such as YouTube, Revver, Viddler, and Vimeo. Once you've created your video, you can send it to those sites and people will start watching it. The more video websites you submit your videos to, the more traffic you'll receive. It's that simple.

Here's another tip: Put your website link in the end of the video, so when people watch it and want to know more about you, they can find you.

A video is a fantastic way for people to connect with you and begin associating trust with your name and, of course, a great way to send more traffic to your website for free.

Secret Weapon Online Strategy #2: Creating Content for Your Blog Site

There's quite a lot of computer terminology out there that confuses people. You may have heard the terms blog or blogging. Basically, a blog is a cleverly designed website that can help you drive more traffic to your primary website.

Don't be alarmed by the name. I, too, felt strange about it until I realized how powerful the technology was. Blogs resemble normal websites except they give you the added facility to easily update your own content.

If they're set up correctly, blogs can be a powerful source of both traffic and sales. The added benefits are that they're free to use and only take a few minutes to set up. Here are some ways you can use a blog site:

- To create a high volume of free website traffic
- To boost your online profile and awareness
- To position yourself as an authority in your industry
- To build a constant stream of leads to your business

I believe blogs are one of the best ways to drive free traffic to your website. There are a lot of people who have started a small blog site and started writing about their passion. Today some of those people are successfully generating millions of visitors per month to their primary site and monetizing that traffic.

> *If you're passionate about your industry, blogs are a great way to attract free traffic to your primary site and monetize that traffic.*

How do you create a blog? It's easy!

Did you know that you can set up a free blog in less than three minutes? It's true!

Here are four steps to set up your first blog:

1. Go to wordpress.com.
2. Create your free account.
3. Enter the requested information.
4. Click Next and you're done.

How simple was that?

Now that you have your blog set up, the next step is to frequently create articles for it. A blog with only a few articles won't attract much traffic. Therefore, the trick is to organize your time so that you allow a few minutes each day to write an article about your industry.

Once you get into the habit of writing blog articles, it'll become second nature to you. Because search engines love the content on your blog, they'll send free traffic to your site.

> *If your blog becomes so successful that you draw thousands of new visitors every day, then you'll be in a great position to monetize the traffic. One of the ways to do that is with blog advertising.*

So what are the various blog advertising, revenue-generating products? There are many, but currently the most popular are Google Adsense and its affiliate products and advertising banners. When you receive a high volume of traffic, a certain percentage of those people will click on the ads on your website. Every time someone new clicks on them, you receive a commission somewhere between $0.10 and $0.30 per click.

This may not conjure up images of retirement on a far-away island off the coast of Portofino, Italy, but if you were to work out the math you'd see that blog advertising is a powerful opportunity for financial freedom. Let's say your website gets 5,000 visitors per day. Out of that 5,000, five percent of them click on your ads. That means that you get paid 5 percent of 5,000, which is $75 per day. If you're in business, you know that cash flow is king. That's $75 per day in completely passive income that you don't work for. It doesn't matter whether you're in the mood to work or not, if you're sleeping, at a party, traveling, sick, or home watching TV. You're going to get paid, regardless! By having that incredible freedom to do whatever you want and still get paid enough to cover your expenses, you'll be financially free. Blog advertising helps you put your financial freedom goals into full swing.

Secret Weapon Online Strategy #3: Writing Articles and Submitting Them to Article Directories

A great way to attract free traffic to your website is to write an informative, valuable article and submit it to an article directory. An article directory is simply a website that contains articles written by people all over the world.

Because search engines love content, if your article is listed in an article directory containing thousands of others with great content, then the search engines will love you, too!

Article directories are a great way to send free, targeted traffic to your site.

There are many article directories out there but the one I recommend the most is Ezine Articles. It's completely free and easy to set up and use.

Here are three steps for setting up your free Ezine Article account today.

1. Go to ezinearticles.com.
2. Create your free account.
3. Fill in the required information.

Once you've successfully created your account, here are some ideas for creating and submitting your first few Ezine Articles:

Study copyright-free, statistical research about your industry. Then create your own copy. Be careful not to plagiarize.

- If you wrote any articles in the past, you can submit them, too.
- You can even write new opinion-style articles for submission.
- You use your existing articles to create an e-book, which you can sell online.
- As you submit more articles, you'll find a direct a correlation to the increase in your site traffic.

Remember, the best thing about these methods is that they are all free and only require your time and passion.

Quick Action Steps

1. Get yourself a digital camera with video capability.
2. Record a 30-second video introducing yourself and what you offer.
3. Download it to your computer.
4. Now upload that video to popular video sites like YouTube and Reever.
5. If you haven't already, create a blog account at wordpress.com.
6. Write one article about your business and post it on your blog.
7. Create a new account at ezinearticles.com.
8. Write one article about your business and post it on Ezine Articles.
9. Remember to place a link to your website at the end of your article.

5

The Five Breakthrough Strategies to Increase Your Website Traffic

I remember a night when I was sitting at a local café. It was around 8 p.m. and I was working on my laptop.

In the past few weeks I noticed that the number of e-mail queries in my inbox was much higher than before. Before, I only received an average of one query every few months as a result of networking at events and seminars. This recent rise to one per week was a huge improvement.

I knew a lot of other web design companies were receiving many queries a day but I was happy that my numbers were improving and that I was moving forward.

I was curious why I was getting more queries so I studied my recent site activity. I did a lot of things on my website like changing the content, uploading new photos, and a few other minor things. However, one thing that sticks out was when I tested out my new search engine optimization (SEO) techniques.

To test whether my SEO techniques were effective, I did a quick search on Google to see if I found my website with a high demand key phrase.

You know what I found?

My website had moved from page 40 to page 2! I couldn't believe my eyes. It was at that point that I finally figured out how to optimize my website for the search engines so that it would be easily detected without breaking any of the rules.

Not only I was happy that I moved to page 2, but I also felt like I'd finally graduated and was part of all the other web design companies that pay several thousands of dollars per month for their own search engine optimization techniques. My technique cost me nothing. It was like my little company was sitting at the "grown-up's" table. It was great.

At that point, I slowly converted that extra traffic to new customers and with my profits I happily invested in a new house, traveled around the world, and gave thousands to charity.

I'm not saying all this to brag. I just want to bring home the power of optimizing your website for the search engines. It doesn't require too much effort or energy, just a little research, implementation, and patience. That extra little tweak on your website could mean the difference between having regular overseas holidays and a yearly holiday.

Tweaking your website just a little bit can change your lifestyle!

Let's play the "What if?" game. What if you got the search engine optimization working well on one website? Once you learn how to do that, why not apply that knowledge to more websites?

Playing the "What If?" Game

1 Website = 1 sale per week @ $97 product = $97

2 Websites = 2 sales per week @ $97 product = $194

3 Websites = 3 sales per week @ $97 product = $291

What if you increased the quality of your marketing and managed to increase one sale to two per week for one website?

1 Website = 2 sales per week @ $97 product = $194

2 Websites = 4 sales per week @ $97 product = $388

3 Websites = 6 sales per week @ $97 product = $582

Tweaking your website could help you save for a deposit on a home, pay off your home or car, fund your travels, your children's education, or your own charity.

Because you've optimized your site well, picture it alongside a high-traffic street with customers walking everywhere.

When I discovered the secrets of website optimization, I immediately applied them to my clients' sites and saw positive results. I managed to massively increase their traffic and sales by simply optimizing their sites.

In this chapter, I cover briefly how I was able to achieve success through optimizing my website. I'm going to give you a bird's eye view on how search engine optimization works.

Debunking the SEO Myths

Before we get into SEO, it's important to understand that it's always changing and that it's important to *always* follow the rules. If you aren't keen on following the rules, then I strongly urge you to put this book down. The reason why I say this is because the search engines are the ones with the power. They have control over how your website is positioned and, if you break any of their rules, you risk your website being de-listed in their searches.

Always follow the SEO rules. Ignore them at your peril.

When I first started my web design company I remember trying for several months to look for my website online. I kept on waiting and eventually couldn't find it no matter which words I searched with.

Finally, out of desperation, I typed in the name of my business to make sure that it was even listed in the search engines. If you can't find your website by typing in a targeted keyword, then the next logical step is to search for your business name to make sure it's even there. My website wasn't even listed under my business name!

The only step left was to search for the actual website link. I typed in my actual website link and there it appeared. This could only mean one thing. My website was banned from the search engines because I was violating some rules.

If you search for your business name or website link in search engines several months after you've submitted it and it doesn't appear, then it's likely that your website has been banned.

After much research, I found out that I was banned from search engines because I was exploiting the rules. As a result, my website never took off, hardly made a profit, and caused my business to later be scrapped.

In the end, if I hadn't learned those lessons with my first business, I wouldn't have made my second website as successful as it is today.

Throughout this book, I cover specific key strategies that I used to get my website listed high in the search engines alongside my biggest competitors. These key breakthroughs and more are discussed later in this book.

Traffic Breakthrough Strategy #1: Domain Name

First I began creating my domain name. My first strategy for a domain name is that it must be short and contain the main keyword. Your domain name is one of the most important pieces of the traffic generation puzzle.

You'll notice that whenever you do a search online for a particular phrase, the domain name plays a big part in the results. I suggest that your domain name is responsible for 60 percent of the results you'll get from optimizing your site. Therefore, you want to invest a lot of time picking the right name and matching it with the appropriate keyword.

> *The quality of your domain name is responsible for around 60 percent of your end results.*

Before picking your domain name, you need to research your market thoroughly and make sure that it's inside a well-defined niche that's hungry for your product or service. The great thing about domain names is that they're inexpensive to purchase and if you pick the wrong one, you can always choose another.

This is much better than investing thousands of dollars into something else with very little return.

Traffic Breakthrough Strategy #2: Website Code

I don't expect you to learn how to write code for your website. If I did, then this book would be about writing code. However, it's important to know what's going on behind the scenes. A lot of web developers neglect to write efficient code and program things haphazardly.

My strategy involves making sure that code is positioned correctly for search engines. In a nutshell, search engines are robots scanning content and, if you're making their job difficult by having "dirty" code, then they won't help you.

I know that sounds strange but it really works. Search engines are the police of the Internet, so make sure you follow their rules. Invest in a good web developer who appreciates clean code and follows high-quality coding standards such as W3C.

Invest in a good web developer now or pay the price later.

Traffic Breakthrough Strategy #3: Website Graphics

You need to measure how fast your website loads with a very slow connection like dial-up. If it takes a long time to load, you'll lose points with the search engines, as well as a lot of potential customers.

One way you can easily measure your website speed is to grab a watch, load your website, and time how long it takes. Once you figure that out, multiply that number by 3. If the total is greater than 15, you must try your best to reduce that number.

> **The Website Measurement Formula**
>
> A = Your Website Homepage Loading Time
>
> A x 3 = Speed Results
>
> If Speed Results are greater than 15 then you need to work on bringing that number down.

I optimized all my website graphics so they would load up within 3 seconds on even the slowest Internet connections.

Many people have slow connections, but if you do the hard work on speeding up your website for all users, it'll rank better in the search engines.

Traffic Breakthrough Strategy #4: Keyword Rich Content

It's so important to have a lot of content on your website. If you don't, people won't find you online and you'll struggle to get queries.

When you're starting out with your new website, aim to have at least 10 pages of keyword-rich content. For example, if you have a

Keyword-rich content is the backbone of traffic generation.

dog-training business you should have 10 pages with dog-related content like training, grooming, nail clipping, etc. Each of those pages must be optimized with keywords.

Another strategy is to create 10 pages of useful content that you would place on the home page. Each of those pages will contain the best and most valuable information you currently offer. By presenting your best material up front, your visitors will be impressed and quickly see the benefits of working with you.

This method is useful when you're creating a blog. Many blogs contain key articles known as "pillar content." Pillar content is designed to give your readers the best information possible and is a great way to make a good first impression.

By having as much content as possible on your website targeted to various niche keywords, your website will have an advantage over other websites that don't understand how visitors and search engines work.

Traffic Breakthrough Strategy #5: Website Linking

A major component of making your website rank high with search engines is ensuring your website is linked to related websites.

When your website details and link are displayed on a like-minded website, this will not only bring targeted traffic to you but will also boost your popularity online.

Think of this as voting. If 10 people voted for you and two people voted for your competitor, then who would be an ideal choice in the industry? The final secret is to make sure you get a lot of votes from various websites that relate to your industry.

I slowly built a lot of links to my websites from my clients' sites. You can build links to your site by simply emailing website owners who are in your industry and ask them to list a link to your site and in return, you list a link to theirs on your own site.

Build your links slowly and your website rankings should increase over time.

Quick Action Steps

Answer these questions.

1. Grab a watch and time how long it takes for your site to load. Does it take longer than 15 seconds?
2. Are there any large video, animation, or music files that take a long time to load? If so, could you do without them or reduce those file sizes to improve speed?
3. Does your home page contain lots of content?
4. Do the additional pages on your site contain a lot of content? How many pages are there?
5. Do your website pages contain the keywords you want people to find you with?

If you answered "no" to any of the questions, spend the next 15 minutes working on their solutions.

6

The Riches Are
in the Niches

S everal years ago, a particular ad in the newspaper caught my attention. It was a free business expo that was being held in a few weeks' time. It caught my attention because during that time, I was building my business and thought that if I attended that expo, I would get some great ideas.

Weeks went by and finally the day came. I went to the expo, visited many booths, and saw what people were selling. A lot of people were selling business improvement services, franchises, and all sorts of other industry products and services.

I remember one booth clearly. The man hosting the booth asked me to drop my business card in a fish bowl in exchange for a small gift. A few days later, my mobile phone rang and it was from the business expo store that I gave my business card to.

They invited me to a free workshop designed to help entrepreneurs improve their businesses. This is where I met a guy named Joe. Joe had been running a business for over 10 years selling trees and plants to his customers and other businesses. We chatted and exchanged a few ideas. Joe was a down-to-earth person and easy to talk to. We traded business cards and that was that.

A few months later, he phoned me. He needed a website for his business. I proceeded to help him build his website and promote his services online.

A few weeks after the site was launched, there was an explosion of traffic on his site. Not only was his website was generating a lot of traffic, but he also got many queries a day. Each one resulted in a sale and his business increased dramatically because of how his website was functioning.

I'm not saying this to brag, and there's a point to my story. After considering the launching of Joe's website a success, I started analyzing why my efforts created such exceptional results for his site, compared to my other clients' sites that generated average results. After all, I applied the same strategies to all my client websites. Why did Joe's website get better results than my other clients? The reason is this: It was all in his niche.

You see, Joe was in the business of selling trees and plants. People sell trees and plants in every state, but Joe's niche was fruit trees and was not being addressed by the competitors in his state. Therefore, that niche was ripe for an opportunity to dominate the market.

Not only did his niche have little competition, but he also had a hungry market. There were many people searching for different ways to plant trees in his area, not to mention they were specifically looking for information on fruit trees.

To explain it further, this is the breakdown of Joe's niche with approximate searches.

Trees (1 million searches per month)

Fruit Trees (500,000 searches per month)

Fruit Trees in [State] (18,000 searches per month)

If his website was targeting "trees" you can be assured he was fighting against millions of online competitors selling trees. Search results in the millions are a good indicator that there's a hungry market out there.

If there's a hungry market for the general category of "trees," then you can be certain that there's also a hungry market for the subcategory of "fruit trees." If you were to target selling "fruit trees in [your state]" then you would define your market in a niche that's hungry. When your keyword search is an extension of several keywords it is called a "long-tail keyword."

> *You must always target a hungry niche and feed that market with the goods it craves.*

A great technique for figuring out the demand of your market is using keyword research tools online. Simply go online and type in "free keyword research tools" and you'll see a list of free tools you can use to study your market.

By taking that extra time to study your market, finding a niche in that market and ensuring that it's hungry for what you're offering, there'll be a greater chance in succeeding online. If the average Joe can do it, so can you!

Secrets of Domain Names Exposed!

Did you know that most domain names out there are incorrectly named for their target markets? I know that's a bold statement, but it's true. If your domain name doesn't reflect your business well enough, the people searching for what you offer won't find you.

Let me give you an example. Let's say that you want to search for car services in New York and there are approximately 1,000 car services there. Each of them has websites named after their businesses, with names like xyzcars.com, abccarservice.com, and 123servicecar.com.

What would you do if you were searching for car services in New York? Would you type in a business name or "car service" and the name of your geographic area? I'm sure you'd type in the latter. The reason why people do this is that it's human nature to search for things that way.

Therefore, if you wanted to increase traffic on your website, why would you just stick with one domain name that had your business name as your domain name? I'm certainly not suggesting you scrap your current domain name.

The reality is that it can cost as little as $100 to register a new domain name with hosting included. What would it take to create a brand new domain name that hits your target market search results and duplicates your website on top of that? Not much at all. Why not create another website that has a proper domain name with a sole purpose of generating leads and let your other domain name be your brand?

That's the power of domain names. What you decide to name your domain plays a very important role in your search engine positioning.

The Steps to Creating the Ultimate Domain Name

There are only two things you need to do to create the ultimate domain name: research your market and register your domain name.

Research Your Market

Simply go to your favorite search engine and type in "free keyword research tools" and there'll be a list of free tools that will enable you to research what people are typing into the search engines. Google offers a great free keyword research tool called "Google Keywords." When you use the tool, make sure you type in your industry and geographic area. For example, "dog training on Mars" and "dog training in New York" will yield different results, which probably indicates where the need for dog training is greater.

You'll learn quite a bit about your market. Make sure you target a hungry audience and popular keywords that have a niche. If you're targeting "dog training" you can be assured that your website will be fighting an uphill battle from day one. But if you're targeting "dog training in [your state]," your competition would be much lower and easier to dominate.

Register Your Domain Name

This next part is easy. Once you've found a popular keyword that's searched by many people and it's niched, the next step is to register that domain name so you own it. You can register domain names for under $100 and it only takes a few minutes online. You need to check to see if the name is available before you register it. For example, if you found that a lot of people were searching for "dog training on Mars" then an ideal domain name would be dogtraining-mars.com if you were targeting people on a planetary scale. If you were targeting the UK market for dog training on Mars, it would read dogtrainingmars.co.uk.

Long-Tail Markets and How to Find Them

When you create a new domain name, you must make sure that it's well defined inside a niche. For example a category like "money" would be a huge market. But if you were to go deeper into its niche, you'd find that there are variations that help specify the target like "make money," "make money online," "make money online ads," and "make money online ads banners."

The idea behind long-tail markets is that 99 percent of the time, the biggest category would be the most competitive and hardest to dominate and break into. The reason is because of its huge market size and the number of people in that market. However, if you target a lower niche market, you'll find it less competitive and easier to dominate. Therefore, it's recommended to create domain names that target long-tail markets.

In my experience, a great way to reflect your niche industry in your domain name is to place the name of your geographic area after the name of your industry. For example, "dog training" can be distilled

Focus on long-tail markets and build your domain name to match that market.

down to "dog training mars." This makes your website a likely catch when someone types in "dog training services on mars." However, you must also make sure that inside your niche, there's a hungry market. There's no point in dominating a market if there aren't any customers!

A Last Note on Domain Names

Make sure that when you register your domain name you do so honestly and ethically. Make sure it's under your name or business name. Don't just register a domain name because you find that there's a hungry market and it's completely outside your business expertise area or something that you'll never target. It's just common decency to let others who are seriously interested in that industry have a chance to grab that domain name.

There have been plenty of times when I needed to purchase a domain name for my service and found that someone else had purchased it years ago with no intention of using it. These people are commonly referred to as *squatters* and they hoard the best domain names in hopes of selling them for a profit.

Quick Action Steps

1. What are the primary keywords you want people to use to find you? Make sure they're narrowly defined and not general like "dogs." A good starting point would be to use your keyword and geographic location.
2. Log on to Google Keywords and type in your primary keywords. The keywords that produce the best results reveal your hungry market.
3. Once you've figured out your keywords, why not create a new domain name with your most important keywords in it. Keep your domain name under 13 characters.

4. Once you've created your domain name, ask your developer to set up a basic blog account on your new domain.

This new website will be your free traffic generator. It should contain your niche articles, ideas, and tips. By loading this new website with your main keywords, you'll attract traffic to it and provide valuable information to your target audience. Don't forget to have a call to action on this website, whether it's to contact you, link to your main website, or purchase your product.

7

How to Increase Your Website Popularity

Before we cover websites you must first understand how search engines see them. Remember that the search engines are not human beings and they use complex algorithms to calculate whether a website is popular or simply a shop in the middle of the desert.

How do search engines view websites?

Whenever I build a website for my clients I always watch it carefully to see how quickly and why it rises up in the search engines. It takes a few weeks to a few months for most of them to rise up or even be seen in the searches. Though their patterns differ, after creating over 100 websites from scratch, I've noticed a common pattern that all search engines tend to use.

To understand this common pattern you must first understand how websites are seen by a computer.

What is a website, actually? It is simply a number of files stored on a computer. That computer is connected to the Internet. Since the computer is connected to the Internet, it's also using an Internet service provider, similar to the one you are possibly paying for now. Most people who have an Internet connection are paying for that service through an Internet service provider, commonly called an ISP.

Because your computer is connected to the Internet, it has an identity called an IP address. Think of your IP address as your DNA. In the same way that no one else has your particular DNA sequence, your IP address similarly defines you. It is unique to you.

The reason why each computer has an IP address is because that's the only way each computer can be identified online. If I wanted to find someone online, all I would need is his or her IP address. It would help me find their ISP and they would have information about the person who's paying for the Internet, which would lead me to the person who owns the computer registered to that account.

Every time someone visits your website, it's possible to see their IP address. A typical IP address would look something like this: 203.109.209.233.

A lot of websites have tracking software embedded in their code. With tracking software you can gather a lot of information about who's visiting your website. You can find what countries they are surfing from, the time of day or night they are viewing your website, and how long they stay on it.

Google has great tracking software called Google Analytics. See the appendix for the web address.

One way the search engines register your website's popularity is by tracking how many different IP addresses it receives visits from. Remember that each IP address has one unique computer associated with it, so it's a good way to track how many people click on your website. The more people who click on your website, the more popular it gets and the higher it rises in the search engines.

What if you were to click on your own website? Because your computer has its own IP address, that address would be recorded every time you visit your website. If you click on your website 100 times, your IP address would be listed in the search engine records 100 times.

Search engines will know that it's you clicking on your own website. This will give you a poor search engine ranking. The search engines differentiate things like this with their log keeping.

This is what a search engine log looks like when the same computer keeps viewing a website.

203.109.209.233
203.109.209.233
203.109.209.233
203.109.209.233
203.109.209.233
203.109.209.233
203.109.209.233
203.109.209.233

But what if you have more than one computer in your home and use each of them to click on your website? Two computers using the same Internet connection share the same IP address.

The search engines know that different people are clicking on your website when they see a list of different IP addresses in their logs. As you can see in the figure list below, all the IP addresses are different, which means they came from different people.

203.139.105.023
203.149.200.209
203.123.029.198
203.160.100.101
203.128.128.144
203.221.199.154
203.211.123.111
203.123.224.224
203.223.122.101
203.168.176.171
203.198.169.123
203.161.157.150

I'm not suggesting that you should visit your website from every computer on every Internet service provider to view your website.

This is definitely not the point I'm trying to get across.

What I'm trying to show you is that by understanding this you can begin to harness the power of search engine optimization.

The final point I want to make is that you should keep designing and writing content for your audience, not just for the search engines. We should never try to cheat the system. It's easy to get carried away with search engine optimization and forget about your target audience. If you do cross that line and are optimizing for the search engines, you risk having your website banned or even taken off the search engines.

> *Always write content for your audience, not only for the search engines.*

Massively Increasing Your Website's Popularity

Have you noticed websites that only have a few pages and are ranked high up in the search engines? There are other websites that rank very with so much more content, and it seems that they deserve better rankings.

The reason why these websites get better rankings is because each website is measured by popularity. The way a website is measured by popularity is with page rank.

A *page rank* is a popularity measurement that's calculated by how many people link to your website.

You can view the popularity and page rank of websites by installing page rank software, like Google Toolbar, on your Internet browser. For example, Google measures your website popularity with an order rating up to 10. If you launch a brand new website it will rank 0/10. If you wait a few months or a year, it may climb to 1/10. This happens when your website has passed the one-year mark and has earned a small amount of trust.

This ranking process takes several weeks to several months, and sometimes years to change. Keep in mind that search engines are always changing their algorithms for catching people who cheat the system.

I remember seeing the page rank go from 0/10 to 5/10 on one of the first sites I built in only three short years. It took a lot of time, effort, and testing, but eventually it worked. When your website increases its page rank that's a good indicator that it will also rise up in the search engines.

I remember when my website had a page ranking of 2/10. Then I recorded a video and wrote an article about the video. The video is about increasing your productivity at work or at home. I submitted that video and article to a productivity website that was seen by thousands of visitors.

This attracted a lot of traffic to my website. One week later its rank went from 2/10 to 3/10.

As a result of some articles I posted on my website, it also moved from page 4 to page 3 in the search engines.

If you were to type in a search phrase and click on the link for the first page that comes up, you would most often find that website holding a very good page rank, especially if your search phrase was only one word.

Type "dog" in the search engine, and you'll find a list of websites that rank very high.

If you seriously want to increase your page rank, one of the most powerful ways to do this is to get high-ranking websites to link back to your website. This tells search engines that those popular websites find your website useful and relevant.

It's like a high authority is giving you a recommendation, which really makes you look good.

If you come across a website with a high page rank, you'll find how many people are linking back to it by typing their domain name in Google's search box, with "link:" at the beginning, like this: link: theirdomainname.com. This lists websites with links to them and you can actually see how many people make that website popular.

You want to get as many links back to your website as possible from relevant, popular sites, not just any old site.

> The websites that link to yours must be relevant to increase your rank in the search engines.

A Powerful Secret to Increasing Your Web Page Popularity

Not only do you increase your site popularity by getting high-ranking sites to link to yours, but because the search engines see that the stamp of approval is from high-ranking sites, your credibility improves.

This doesn't mean you should go out there and get any high page ranking website to link to yours. Search engines will discriminate if they see that they're a bunch of irrelevant sites and won't promote you.

Imagine your website is about dogs. If a finance company, a window company, a seafood company, and a pizza company all link to your website, this would not be seen as natural in the search engines eyes. Why? Because those websites are unrelated to yours.

If 10 other websites relating to dogs linked to your website that would be seen as a good indicator your website is popular in the dog industry and would earn you a good page rank.

A good way to get people to put your link on their site is to ask them to do it. Make sure you also link back to them as a courtesy. Keep in mind that these highly ranked sites get lots of requests from people asking for the same thing, so keep your request short and polite, and don't appear too needy.

> People will link to your website only if you provide quality content for their readers.

A good way to coax a link exchange is to put the other site's link onto yours first. Then that website owner places your link on their site in return.

Keep in mind that it's completely up to the website owner, and you should not be pushy. They are doing you a favor, and you should appreciate any response you get. If they find that your website has valuable content, then they may link to you, but if your website doesn't provide valuable content for their readers, it's unlikely that your website will be linked.

How to Use the Power of Website Linking Strategies

One of the best ways to boost your website traffic is to keep using linking strategies. These require no programming experience, special knowledge, cost (most of the time), or big effort on your part.

Search engines also determine whether your website is a relevant search result when they see how popular it is. They measure this by looking at how many people link to your website. So let's say that we have a dog training website that has five websites linking to it. Those websites are of various backgrounds like golf, schools, cars, and a few other random industries.

Does this make the dog training website a reliable source of information if it's being linked from irrelevant sources? Definitely not!

What if the dog training website had 10 dog training websites pointing to it? What is the chance of that dog training website being a reliable source in that industry? Very high!

It's a good idea to get people in your industry to link to your website.

You can get people in your industry to link to your website by e-mailing them. If you e-mail 10 websites asking them to link to yours with a promise of linking back to them, you'll probably get at least one yes. Remember, it doesn't cost money to send an e-mail, just a minute of your time.

If you spent 10 minutes a day requesting link exchanges, by the

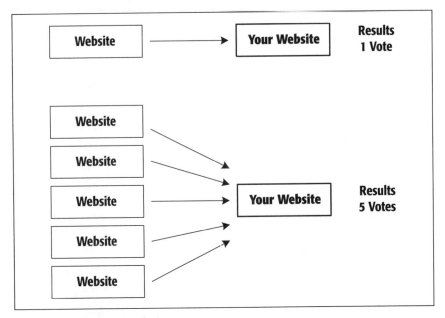

Table 7-1. Website popularity

end of the week you'd have contacted 70 websites and gained seven positive responses. That's seven websites linking to you and boosting your online profile. Your competitors most likely don't have anyone linking to them.

How to Get People to Automatically Link to Your Website

You can actually get people to link to your website without even trying hard. Let's say you create a blog and every week write several useful industry-related articles. This will be valuable to your readers.

When your blog is a source of useful, free information, you'll get a lot of regular and repeat visitors, which in turn, will attract like-minded bloggers.

If those bloggers find your site useful, they'll write about you on their blog and link to you without you knowing it. Once again, this attracts traffic to your site and increases its popularity. You didn't have to ask for it. It automatically happened.

> *If you write quality articles that people find useful, they'll automatically link to you.*

This is how those major websites get millions of hits per day on their blogs. They spend a long time building up an inventory of useful articles until their site picks up enough traffic to be seen by the masses.

The Story of My Website Linking Strategies

I once received an e-mail requesting that I sponsor a local event. It was a cutting-edge web technology event to be sponsored by several million-dollar companies.

This one-time event was to host over 200 web developers and programmers. I immediately volunteered to be a sponsor and as a result, my business was advertised on their t-shirts and websites. I hadn't known much about sponsoring at the time, except that I had always wanted to try it.

I didn't get any business from that event. I realized that my target market was wrong and that programmers and web developers weren't my target clients. However, a few months later, I made a shocking discovery.

My website had jumped up several pages on the search engines and was beating nearly all my competitors. What had happened was that my website gained popularity because of the event that I sponsored. Their site linking to mine made my website hugely popular with the search engines.

That event sponsored website had large numbers of high-profile websites linking to it, which in turn, made them a large website. Because their website earned appreciation from other high-profile websites, my site merely being linked to it caught some of that attention and was also viewed with respect.

As a result of being listed as a sponsor on their main page I received tons of traffic, queries, and of course, sales. Each sale was worth thousands of dollars. You can imagine how much money you could make if you apply the few linking strategies I've outlined here.

The Sandbox Theory

The sandbox theory refers to the idea that newly launched sites are on probation because they don't have any history for the search engines to judge them by. In the early stages of a website's existence, it's unclear whether it'll break or follow the rules, so it has to be on probation until it earns a reputation.

Over the many cycles of building websites, I've found this theory amazingly predictable. One of the first websites I launched was design related. I broke all the rules, placed too many keywords, spammed every page, and did everything possible to try and get ranked high by the search engines using brazen, rule-breaking techniques. It took about a month for that site to get banned. It was never permitted back on the search engines. I broke the rules and didn't play fair.

If it weren't for that experience, I would have never learned how to place both my own and my clients' niche websites on Google's search results front page and generate thousands of dollars as a result.

Remember to check your website's page ranking to try to improve it. If you're dealing with a new website, your ranking will slowly go from 0 to 1. Over the course of a few months it'll increase, but there'll be a barrier midway. As much as you optimize your website, you have to take more action to bring it up to a page rank of 7.

It gets more difficult to bring your page rank closer to the highest level as it incorporates other variables, like the flow of thousands of people linking to you and receiving millions of visitors daily.

You'll notice that major websites like Facebook, Myspace, and Hotmail will have huge page rankings. This is due to the relentless flow of return traffic that they've built over the course of many years.

Those websites command millions of hits every day. It's no mystery why their services are so popular and are ranked so well by the search engines.

Quick Action Steps

1. Find 10 websites that relate to your niche industry. Send them each an e-mail to ask if they're interested in forming a joint venture. Ask them to list your information on their site and offer to do the same for them on your site. The one condition you must ensure is that they use active links that lead to your website.

2. If you haven't done so already, install page rank software, like Google Toolbar, on your web browser. The software you use should contain a page rank feature so you can see how popular your website becomes each time it loads in your browser.

3. Spend a few minutes analyzing your competition by looking at their page ranks and popularity levels. Look at whom they link to and follow those links. If they're linking to an industry website, why not request that industry website link to your site?

On your blog or website, post a pleasant request suggesting readers check out your website if they enjoyed reading your article through the provided link.

8

Unlocking the Secrets Behind Social Networking and Its Traffic Potential

I was honored to be the best man at a wedding a few years ago. I remember seeing cameras flashing everywhere after giving a speech to the wedding party and guests.

As I finished my speech, people congratulated and complimented me on it, commenting that it was one of the best they had ever heard, especially coming from a best man. I was quite hungry from celebrating all day and looking forward to eating and drinking more champagne. As I was walking toward the food table, my phone rang. It was an old friend I hadn't spoken to in awhile.

He immediately asked, "Did you just get married, Khoa?" to which I replied, "No, I'm actually the best man at a friend's wedding. Why do you ask?" He said he had just seen photos of me online in a very sharp suit and blue tie while speaking to a huge audience. There was a bride in the background and everyone was applauding.

I found out that as soon as I had finished speaking, people were taking photographs and uploading them with their cell phones to our mutual friends. Within minutes, everyone in their phone contacts directory knew what I was wearing, where I was, and the color of my tie! Whether that disturbs you is a different subject altogether, but my goal in telling you the story is to emphasize the power of social networking and how you can use it to build massive amounts of targeted traffic.

Welcome to the New World of Social Networking!

Social networking is the current trend of communicating with people online. Over the years the Internet has evolved. Simple websites have slowly turned into smart websites and now you can easily update content on them. Whether you're into social networking or not, this new platform must be taken advantage of.

Over the past few years, the huge rise in technology has enabled people to communicate with each other in new ways. Some of these technologies include blogging and social network sites like Facebook, Myspace, and Twitter, to mention a few. Each of those social networking platforms is connected to its own fan base of human users anywhere from 1,000 to 10,000 large. When the numbers climb higher than that they almost become a news station.

These sites provide their communities with tools to share information online with one another, like photos, personal journal entries about their lives, or anything at all. This power for people to easily post and share their opinions creates a whole type of "news publishing."

Years ago, news agencies were the predominant source of news. Today's news is often captured and broadcast by citizens first. For example, if a shocking global event occurs, news reporters would arrive at the scene, interview witnesses, and at the end of the day, publish the story. However, today people who are exposed to that kind of an event automatically post their photos, video, and ideas about it on social networking sites, where it spreads like wildfire.

This information arrives online seconds after events occur, attracting thousands of comments, which you can easily tap into online with keyword searches.

By understanding how social networking works, you can harness its great power to attract a huge wave of traffic to your site, and then convert that traffic to sales.

Building Relationships Using Social Networking Platforms

Social networking sites like Facebook, Myspace, and Twitter and blog sites operate to a similar end. On each of them the user creates a community to share information with people in it. The power behind creating your own social network community is the instant way a certain level of trust is created, just by being in the same community with others. Those on the receiving end are saying, "You are my friend and I am willing to receive communications from you." This is a powerful formula to increase sales on your website (which I explain later).

Social networking is great way to build stronger relationships with your customers and communicate with them on a more personal level.

Let's say that you create a new social network account on Facebook. Over the next few weeks, you find that the number of friends you now have, compared to the first week you joined, has increased significantly. People find you through their different social circles, or networks, like those of old high school friends or professional circles.

You find whenever you post an idea, your friends respond quickly. You soon realize you have the power to communicate with a large audience any time you like. If you tell them you've just launched a new website, some of your friends will probably visit that site through the link you display. However, in this environment, your network is most likely to consist of friends and family, not customers.

What if you created a social network account dedicated to just customers? Can you do this? You certainly can!

Attracting More Targeted Traffic to Your Site and Increasing Your Sales With Social Networking

If you create a new social networking account dedicated to building a list of customers, you really create an asset for your business. If you have a large list of contacts who are willing to receive communications from you, then using this asset is a good way to grow your business relationships.

Let's suppose that you have 5,000 "fans," "friends," or people in your network and because you've built long-term relationships with them, they consider you a trustworthy advisor. You then launch a new product on your website and tell everyone in your social network to check it out.

Let's say that only 10 percent of 5,000 people actually click on the link. This would result in 500 people visiting your website. If the product you were advertising were priced at $197 and 10 percent of the 500 people purchased your product, that's 50 customers multiplied by $197 and adds up to $9,850 in sales!

That's the power behind social networking; it gives you a means to communicate with your community. However, it's highly recommended that you don't continually "spam" your network with offers because your audience will get sick of it and leave you. The strength of social networking for business is to build a solid relationship with your client base.

There's also a huge difference between someone you don't know and someone who trusts you. If you were to offer a service to 10 strangers you'd find that maybe one or two of them would be interested. However, offering that service to 10 friends who trust you would yield a greater number of interested customers. The reason for this difference is that you already have a relationship with them. Therefore, using social networks to build relationships with your prospects helps increase your conversion rate in selling whatever it is you have to offer.

You need to nurture your network of contacts by giving them useful information, interesting articles, and valuable tips. This may take weeks, months, or years. Because social networking is mostly relationship driven, building great relationships with your community members will reward you financially.

If you look after your community, it will look after you.

Quick Action Steps

1. If you haven't done so already, create a new social networking account. The current popular ones are Facebook, Twitter, and Myspace.

2. Take a few minutes this month to learn how to add members to your network and communicate with them.

3. Start building your social network community by e-mailing clients and friends.

4. Decide today that every month you'll use all of your social networking tools to communicate with your growing community. It should only take a few minutes of your time each month. You can, of course, use them more frequently if you wish.

5. Make sure you offer something of value like a tip or some insights or lessons. Always offer something valuable before you advertise a product.

Focus on building a strong relationship with your community, not selling to them.

9

How to Use Free Publicity to Get Free Traffic and Increase Your Sales

Have you ever received an e-newsletter about a company, event, or service? Of course you have. Even though many people receive these newsletters, they don't realize that those newsletters are a gold mine of free advertising.

Let me explain.

My Newsletter Story

I once received an e-newsletter targeted to local businesses in Western Australia. It contained tips and strategies on public speaking and business success.

Something in the newsletter caught my attention. It was locally produced by a public speaking community with a large database of contacts among small business owners.

The newsletter contained a lot of valuable information on successful public speaking, improving business profits, and marketing tips. Even though it covered a lot about business, it didn't cover much about building effective websites.

I decided to write to the person responsible for putting the newsletter together, whose contact information I found at the bottom of the publication.

Here's the e-mail I wrote:

Hi there,

I just received your newsletter and found it very informative and interesting. Great work!

I noticed that you didn't have features and articles on driving traffic to your website, or any other website-related strategies. Your readers are missing out on a lot of great information in that area.

I specialize in this area and would like to share my knowledge with your readers by writing articles and contributing them to your newsletter free of charge. Are you interested in that?

(No product advertisements, just my name at the bottom.)

Thanks. I look forward to hearing from you soon!

Within 24 hours, I received a positive response from the newsletter producer accepting my offer to contribute.

I then wrote a one-page article targeting their readers, written in their language, featuring much of their terminology. I spent an hour writing a simple, easy-to-understand article with useful information.

The only advertising I displayed was my name at the bottom of the article. If the reader was interested in my article and wanted more information about what I did, they would find my website through a quick online search of my name.

As soon as my article was published and distributed to the newsletter's community members, I received a huge surge of traffic from new sources. I also received tons of queries, some of which eventually resulted in business.

By investing a few minutes in writing an e-mail and an hour writing an article, I attracted some free targeted traffic to my website and increased my sales.

Most newsletter authors are constantly trying to add new, rich content to their newsletters so it continually provides valuable information for their readers. By having an expert contribute to their newsletter for free is highly favorable.

Why Free Publicity Is Important

Getting free publicity is easy. All you have to do is keep your eyes open. Whenever you receive a newsletter and you believe the people sending it match your target market, send an e-mail to the newsletter publisher asking them if you can contribute to it.

It costs nothing and takes only a few minutes of your time. You can even copy my e-mail, just changing the details. As a refresher, each newsletter has approximately between 100 and 1,000 readers. By "advertising" yourself through sharing your knowledge, you position yourself as an authority in your field. When you do that people will come to you for advice.

It's also really important that you prepare a list of topics to write about. This will make it easier to write if you encounter writer's block. See Figure 9-1 on the next page for how this works.

A good rule of thumb is to contact at least 10 newsletters each day. You only need to start working with one newsletter to reap great rewards. Each month, you'll receive a large amount of traffic for free. Make sure you submit your best five articles during the initial stage. You want to start off on the right foot with the best information you have to offer.

Remember that you're trying to build a solid relationship with your newsletter partner and readers. Always write quality, content-rich articles that really help your readers. There's no point in writing something that people don't value. If they don't value your work, they won't contact you. It's that simple.

Contact at least 10 industry-relevant newsletter publishers daily.

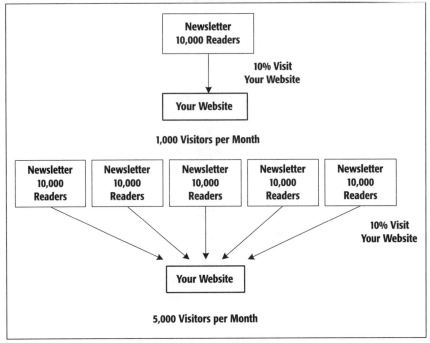

Figure 9-1. The Power of Free Publicity—The Newsletter Strategy

Always keep a lookout for free publicity media channels; they're a gold mine.

Where Can You Find Free Publicity?

There are many opportunities to contribute to a community and receive free publicity. Here are some of them:

- Newsletters
- Associations
- Small magazines
- Communities
- Offline flyers

Do a search for community publications in your area. The possibilities are endless!

Keep an Archive of Quality Articles Ready for Use

Since you must discipline yourself to write an article each month, it's a good idea to keep a bank of article drafts, complete with outlines so that you can finalize them when needed.

Build a newsletter article drafts bank.

There will be some days that you don't want to write and that's normal. If you feel like that, you can always make a withdrawal from your article drafts bank.

Writing Articles for Publicity Guidelines

I always find that you should follow a system when you write your articles. Here are some guidelines that help me write quality articles:

1. Always know to whom you're writing. Define whether they are public speakers, corporations, business owners, etc.
2. Write to them as if you were speaking to them in person.
3. Change your language so that it suits your target audience. If they're dog trainers, you would use terms that relate to them. Use pictures and stories they can relate to. If you're explaining something complicated, use analogies of familiar scenarios.
4. Always have a treat in each article. It should be something they can take away and use.
5. Keep it easy to understand and read. Break up your article so it's easy to digest. For example, turn large blocks of text into paragraphs and bulleted lists.
6. Never advertise directly or make your article a sales pitch. Nothing turns people off more than a salesperson pretending to offer free advice. If do this, you'll lose the respect of your readers and newsletter partner. If you write a good enough article, don't worry, people will find you online, so make sure you have your website ready.

Gaining free publicity is a fantastic way to attract quality traffic to your website and increase your sales.

Quick Action Steps

1. Find 10 potential media outlets you can form a joint venture with. This could be an online website, industry magazine, or a contact with a large database.
2. Send an e-mail to those outlets offering to contribute to their newsletter or association for free.
3. Once you've secured at least one outlet, congratulations are in order. Now begin writing quality, informative, and valuable content every month.

Build a strong relationship with your new joint venture and respect their conditions. Don't write about your product. Focus on writing about tips and strategies that'll help your target market. If they're interested in learning more about your business, then they'll seek you out.

10

Six Fast Website Changes You Can Apply Immediately

H ave you ever visited a website and closed it within a few seconds?

There are many reasons why people do this. A guest will want to leave your website when it:

- Takes too long to load
- Doesn't look like it relates to what they're searching for
- Doesn't load correctly
- Is too cluttered
- Is too empty

There are so many reasons why people click off your website. If you think about it, why invest thousands of dollars in building it when visitors just tune out?

Solving click-off is one of the biggest problems I've discovered when it comes to building a successful website.

Therefore, I've devised six fast ways to dramatically improve your website's performance, speed, and results.

Fast Website Change #1: Speed Up Your Website

I have a rule when it comes to designing effective websites that keeps your visitors on your site. I call it the 8-Second Speed Rule.

If a visitor comes to your website and within eight seconds they leave, that tells you that you need to fix something. The home page is the most important part of your website because it's the "hook" that gets people to stay and continue reading.

Your homepage should captivate every visitor for longer than eight seconds.

If people arrive at your home page, you need to somehow grab their attention, keep them on your site, and get them to take action. Otherwise, you've wasted a good lead that could have become a great long-term customer.

Here are some of my strategies to get people hooked onto your website:

- Your website must load faster than fifteen seconds on a slow Internet connection.
- Arrange your homepage content so that people look from left to right and scan downward.
- Have a large eye-catching image at the top of your website so that it grabs people's attention. A close-up picture of a person usually does the trick.
- Have lots of content on your homepage but make sure you break it up using bullet points, images, and headings. No one wants to read a large block of text on your website.
- At the very bottom of every page, including your home page, have your call-to-action link. Usually this is a link to your Contact Us page.
- Make the website visually appealing but also clean and simple to read. I find black text on white background always works.

Optimizing Your Website Graphics

One of the biggest contributors to a slow-loading website is large, high-quality images. If you have a web page with a lot of images, then chances are high it will take a long time to load and, as a result, you'll lose visitors.

Another big contributor to slow loading is large animations. Think of those animations as a collection of images that need to each load. If you feature an animation that can contain over 100 high-quality images on your site, it would take a very long time to load up.

Optimizing your website graphics requires skills with specific software and you may need to contact your web designer or developer to do this for you. Make sure that your website home page, which is the most important page on your entire site, does not contain too many photos or fancy animation.

An easy way to test the speed of your website is to view it on a slow Internet connection. If you don't have access to a slow connection, type "website speed tester" into your favorite search engine and you'll find a long list of free tools to test the speed of your site.

Why Search Engines Love Fast Sites

Search engines are very smart. They seem to know which site is good for the end user and which isn't. One thing search engines love is fast websites. If you tried to view a website and it took 20 minutes to load, would you wait for it? Of course not!

Visitors and search engines love fast websites.

Search engines know you use them to find great websites and if the choices they offer have tedious loading times you'll go elsewhere. You won't bother using that search engine again and you'll choose another one next time. Search engines know you're looking for sites relevant to your search that don't waste your time. Therefore, it's imperative to always time your website loading speed. If it loads slowly on a fast Internet connection, you need to speed it up.

Fast Website Change #2: Switch to Faster Hosting

With one of the host providers I tried, I noticed that after I'd uploaded all the files to my site each page loaded very quickly. One day, I came across an ad that said, "Hosting—only $50 per year!" I noticed that it was about $50 cheaper than the one I was using so I thought I'd try the cheaper option, since hosting is all the same, right? Wrong!

Once I uploaded all the files and spent nearly the entire day configuring the website, I tested the loading speed on my newly purchased host.

It was extremely slow. Each page took eight seconds to load. My website was previously loading in three seconds and now it was taking 11 seconds! I thought to myself that perhaps the reason why the hosting is so cheap is because it's stored on slow computer servers. I decided to ignore it and just leave the website on the new server for a while.

A few weeks later, I noticed that my website had dropped in search engine rankings. It used to rank high in the searches, but now had dropped several pages. Not only that, but my traffic had greatly decreased because I was so far away from the front page search results. As a result, I noticed that many people clicked off my website immediately because it loaded so slowly.

From that day forward, I realized that I may have saved myself $50 in hosting expenses but lost thousands of dollars worth of business. Always pick a good, reputable web host known for fast, high-quality connections. You'll reap the rewards later.

Fast Website Change #3: Bolding Your Keywords

You can gauge the amount of traffic that some of the bigger websites out there are getting by the number of ads they display. Pay attention to the way these sites focus on providing informative, high-quality content pertinent to their users. You'll also notice that they bold the keywords you used to find them with in the search engine.

The search engines want to provide you with websites that are the most relevant to your search and have the highest quality content they can find.

That makes it critical for you to provide the most relevant, high-quality information your target market will be searching for. One way I connect my users to that great information is to bold the words they were searching for on my web pages.

For example, if someone were to search for "cycling in Perth" I would make sure that my website has the keywords "cycling" and "Perth" in boldface. I'm not suggesting that you bold *all* your website keywords. Just make sure you bold one or two keywords close to the top of your web page. I found that single technique truly effective in search engine optimization.

Not only is displaying keywords in boldface type a great way to attract search engines, but it also makes it easier for your users to find the keywords on your pages, and isn't that important as well?

People like scanning websites for their particular search phrase. When a viewer sees their search words boldfaced on your site, it's more likely they'll scroll down and read more. If you're using software to update content on your website, you can easily bold a keyword by highlighting the text and clicking the standard boldface "B" button on the interface. You can even ask your web developer to do this for you.

Fast Website Change #4: Tagging Your Graphics

Another way to attract more traffic to your website is to optimize your graphics so they become more visible to the search engines. We all know that when you search Google for a particular key phrase, it provides a list of results that closely relate to your search. You may have also used the image searching feature that lets you type in a search phrase like "dog training" and view a list of related images.

Many people don't realize how much they can benefit from being listed in the Google images database. I've personally generated a lot of traffic by being listed there when people are searching for images. It's definitely proven to be a valuable resource for attracting traffic to my sites.

So how do people find you when they search for images? It's easy.

When you're building your website, make sure your web designer includes the correct coding to hook your images with relevant keywords.

I don't want to scare you with technical mumbo jumbo, so I'm only going to describe how optimizing your images can attract more traffic to your website.

In the box below there are two lines of web code. One has been optimized and the other has not.

Optimized Image

<img src="dog_training_with_angela.jpg" title="A picture of Angela training a dog in New York" alt="Angela is showing you how you can train your dog" />

Non-Optimized Image

<img src="pic1.jpg" />

Let's start with the non-optimized image. When a search engine looks for images, it needs to check the code to find out what that image is all about.

If I were to use the words "dog training in new york" to search the images database, there is nothing in that code that relates to my search. First of all, the image file is named "pic1.jpg," which doesn't describe what the image is, so it's useless. As for the optimized image, you can see that the file name is more descriptive. "Dog_training_with_angela.jpg" is much more definitive than "pic1.jpg."

If I were to send you those two images, and you only saw their names without opening them up, which one would tell you what it looks like? The search engines need clues as to what the image is and, if you rename them so they're more descriptive, then your images will rise up in the database search results.

Make sure your images are named descriptively in your code.

Notice there other two other parts to the code, named "title" and "alt."

Graphic Tags: The Alt Tag

Have you ever moved your mouse over an image, left it there for a few seconds and then, all of a sudden, a little text appears over the image describing what it is?

The purpose of this little feature is to make it easy to see more information about a particular image. It also helps people who have visual trouble finding and seeing images.

For example, if you have a photo of yourself that was taken in front of a mountain, you could include specific information about it such as "Here I am in front of Austria's mountains in 1992 before we went whitewater rafting."

Of course, the main content on your website can include more information if you wish, but if you want to include specific information about the image, then it's useful to use those two tags "title" and "alt."

Graphic Tags: The Title Tag

The title tag is similar to the alt tag. The only thing you really need to know about it is that it provides more information about the image when it loads up. It's important to use a good description of the image that contains relevant keywords.

A Warning About Keyword Stuffing

When optimizing your images, don't stuff keywords continuously into your code. The search engines will know you're trying to cheat the system and break the rules, and you'll run the risk of becoming banned from their listings.

The following box shows an example of keyword stuffing:

```
<img src="dog_training_dog_training_dog_training.jpg"
title="dog training dog training dog training dog training"
alt="dog training dog training dog training dog training dog
training" />
```

As you can see, this image code is crammed with as many key-words as possible to hook the term "dog training." That won't work, though, because the search engines can easily see this is key word spamming and will blacklist the website.

Finally, as a good rule of thumb, it's important to describe each image without spamming the image with too many keywords. It'll work against you. Describe the image correctly and your website will take care of the rest.

Don't spam or overload your web pages or images with too many keywords or you'll get banned.

Fast Website Change #5: Update Your Website Dates

I've always noticed that a website has a better chance of being indexed on search engines when the date at the bottom is current. When your website has the current date, it's basically telling the visitors that this website is up to date. It's fresh and current.

The search engines know this and take it into consideration. After all, search engines want to provide you with the best possible results.

First Impressions Count

If you visited a website and scrolled to the bottom and saw "copyright 1991," what would you think? I don't know about you, but I'd think the last time that website had been updated was in 1991. Outdated information makes the site look neglected and unprofessional. If a website has been neglected, it's clear that the owner doesn't care about the contents so why should anyone bother reading more?

Knowing that, what would happen if a viewer visited your site right now? Would they see current data or stale information that's one, two, or even three years old?

Why Dates Are Important

We all know that search engines and visitors love updated, relevant information. By making sure your copyright date is current, you tell search engines and visitors that your website has been updated recently. It also demonstrates that your website is looked after frequently.

Fast Website Change #6: Follow W3C Compliance

In a nutshell, W3C compliance is an online standard, or set of rules, that, when followed, makes your website look like it's been carefully put together. For example, when you see packaged food at the grocery store that displays approval seals, you know they've been rigorously inspected and made by following certain guidelines.

The job of W3C compliance is to make sure websites adhere to a strict quality standard. When you create your site according to these standards it tells the world you care about quality and taking good care of your site.

Follow W3C compliance standards.

When you follow the W3C compliance, you make sure all your code is correctly put together and follows their website programming rules.

For example, I may use code like this to display an image:

```
<img src="images/image.jpg">
```

This would work fine on most browsers; however, if you want to follow W3C compliance standards, you need to correctly write the code. The correct way of doing that looks like this:

```
<img src="images/image.jpg" />
```

Do you notice a difference? It's the slash at the end of the code. I know this may seem tedious, like it doesn't relate directly to getting more traffic; however, this is an example of not following online rules. If you break rules, you'll be penalized.

My own experience showed me that if I made the extra effort to follow these standards, my site earned better rankings than others that didn't spend that extra time.

Let's say that you're a cop meeting two new people at a crime scene. One person doesn't follow the rules and the other does. Which one are you going to immediately favor?

You don't need to learn the intricate details of writing code to follow W3C compliance. You do need to know that it's important for increasing traffic on your site and adding the clout that shows it was built with high standards.

Next time you're hiring a new web developer or speaking with your existing one, make sure they're applying W3C compliance to all of their website work.

Quick Action Steps

1. Load your website. Does it load faster than eight seconds? If not, think of ways to make it load faster. Could you remove the animations, delete irrelevant video, or reduce the large images to smaller file sizes? Is your host part of the problem?
2. Does your website have a good balance of content and graphics? Is there too much text? Are there too many graphics? Balance your website by equalizing that balance.

3. Do you display your main keywords at the top of your Web page in boldface? Pick one main keyword near the top of the page and boldface it.

4. Ask your designer/developer to tag and rename all the graphics in your code with the proper descriptions.

   Make sure your website date at the bottom of your site is current.

11

The Shocking Truth
About Your Website Code

I know you may not want to hear this, but the way a website is coded and positioned does help increase your website traffic. In my personal experience, by writing effective code you can increase the loading speed of your website.

Let's say that your website code looks like this:

> Lorem ipsum dolor sit amet, consectetur adipiscing elit. Praesent vitae orci id purus tristique euismod. Suspendisse orci tortor, vehicula placerat auctor in, luctus et nulla. Cum sociis natoque penatibus et magnis dis parturient montes, nascetur ridiculus mus. Quisque justo nisl, porttitor id facilisis eget, malesuada vel dui. Suspendisse pharetra metus nec sapien iaculis quis mattis dui pulvinar. Vivamus in eros in ante ullamcorper consectetur ac ac libero. Quisque facilisis, **sed do eiusmod** fringilla, justo leo aliquet lorem, vel tempor nulla ac metus. Aliquam

Figure 11-1. Non-optimized Website Code

Were you able to find the bold text in that block of code? Don't be concerned about interpreting the nonsense text; imagine what it's like for search engines to go through your website and find relevant information.

Imagine what it would look like if you asked your web developer to clean up, or optimize, the code. Here's what that same code would look like after it was optimized:

Maecenas bibendum ipsum sit amet tortor mattis in consectetur **adipisicing elit**, nunc ullamcorper. Cum sociis natoque penatibus et magnis dis parturient montes, nascetur ridiculus mus. Aliquam eu lorem eget sem dictum tincidunt. In dictum felis in nulla iaculis ut rutrum erat lacinia. Mauris gravida lorem fringilla felis ultrices et sodales dolor volutpat. Quisque tristique

Figure 11-2. Optimized Website Code

Notice how much easier it is to find information in smaller amounts of code? If your website code was simplified and written effectively, it would be more favorable to search engines. This is because it tells the search engine that your web developer cares about your website and doesn't write haphazardly.

If your web developer cares about your site, it means that your site is geared for its visitors. That makes the search engines appreciate you more because you're aligned with their business vision of providing the most relevant search results to the audience.

Optimize your code to make it easier for the search engines robots to crawl your site.

In the world of software development, there are many ways to display page features, whether they are graphics, copy, or video. There are different ways to code them and it can get pretty technical, but all you need to focus on is making sure that the developer you choose has a neat, clean coding style so the search engines will love you.

Here are some questions to ask your web developer to make sure that their coding isn't sloppy:

1. Do you follow W3C-compliant coding standards?
2. Do you prefer "div tags" over "tables"?
3. Do you centralize repetitive code in a single file instead of making changes to all the pages?

If your web developer understands those questions and has answered yes to at least one of them, then he or she is a good coder.

Another point I need to mention is that most Web designers don't know how to write code. They only know how to design websites. They usually have no interest in coding or care how it's written, just as long as it displays their creativity. So be careful when choosing a web designer.

Good Coding Practices: W3C Compliance

One of the best ways to be immediately favored by the search engines is to make sure your code is W3C compliant. It's similar to the military. As you get promoted, you earn a rank. If your website is coded using W3C compliance rules, your website will be seen as a "captain" in your niche.

Templates, Templates, and More Templates

Have you ever seen those website templates that you can purchase for $49 or under? They may look nice but in my experience, the coding behind them is a disaster waiting to happen.

There are many website templates out there that you can purchase for a small fee. The problem with them is that they lookugly to the search engines and will be a pain for your web developer to change. They'll also end up costing you more money in the long run.

I once had a client who needed me to make changes to the website template that he had purchased for $80. I wasn't a fan of those templates, but I decided to help him. Here's what I learned from that experience:

- Never again work with website templates.
- It takes more time to make changes to a template than to build from scratch.
- It wastes money.
- It wastes time.
- It didn't benefit the client because it never ranked high in the search engines.
- The client didn't receive any traffic and, as a result, any sales either.

I find it best to build a website from the ground up instead of using a template that was built by someone who doesn't care about programming.

Location, Location, Location

We all know this is key to the real estate market. If you purchase a property in a great location, then the likelihood of a rise in value is high. Just as with real estate, the location of your website code is important.

When a search engine scans your website code, it goes from top to bottom. As it's scanning, the software algorithm makes sure the content is relevant to whatever the visitor was searching for.

For example, if you were in the business of dog training and all your keywords were positioned at the bottom of your site; Figure 11-3 shows what it would look like to the search engines:

What does this tell the search engines? If your website's primary goal is to provide dog training services, then why would you provide your primary goal at the end of your website? It just doesn't seem relevant to what people are searching for.

If you were to structure your website code so that the most important keywords and primary goals are closer to the top, then it would look like that shown in Figure 11-4.

In et lorem sem, ut faucibus arcu. Nunc metus neque, laoreet sed faucibus hendrerit, malesuada vitae arcu. Maecenas sit amet ipsum eros, ac hendrerit est. Morbi tincidunt fermentum hendrerit. Donec eget tristique felis. Quisque mattis auctor dolor vel sodales. Pellentesque et nunc urna. Nullam id ipsum quis arcu ultrices elementum eu vitae tellus. Aliquam mi eros, convallis at varius vitae, ornare ut neque. Aliquam aliquet, lectus eget posuere feugiat, tortor velit feugiat risus, vel ornare enim risus **dog training** eget sem. Curabitur nunc nibh, vulputate mollis **dog training** blandit at ante. In **dog training** condimentum orci, quis faucibus erat

Figure 11-3. Primary Keywords Buried in Code

Integer **dog training** euismod, mi non consectetur mattis, erat ipsum mattis velit, ut **dog training** mattis **dog training** risus mi euismod erat. Vestibulum ante ipsum primis in faucibus orci luctus et ultrices posuere cubilia Curae; Nam accumsan, diam eget dignissim posuere, tortor risus tristique orci, at ullamcorper eros neque in nulla. Aliquam sed euismod urna. Maecenas tincidunt aliquam adipiscing. Donec aliquet risus vel purus varius mollis. Nunc suscipit fringilla erat, sed egestas odio ornare vitae. Cras at enim lorem. Fusce vulputate tellus a sapien vulputate egestas. In placerat magna et lectus aliquam nec bibendum arcu vulputate. Curabitur ac tincidunt gue.

Figure 11-4. Positioning Your Primary Keywords at the Top

As you can see in this figure, the search engine would now know that this website's primary goal is dog training and therefore relevant to the visitor's search.

> *Structure your website code so that your main keywords are closer to the top of the page.*

It's important to push your most important assets to the top of your website so they seem relevant to the search results. I've done this several times for my clients and watched their sites beat the competition and climb to the #1 search results position.

Remember not to use only keywords at the top of the website; that would be considered spamming. The search engines would ban you for that. Sprinkle just a few keywords in at the top of your site.

Powerful Meta Tags That Drive Your Online Success

Meta tags are a powerful way to increase your traffic. Your website rankings will drop significantly compared to another website that has them.

Meta tags are a special coding technique located at the top of every web page. They help determine what your content is about and usually contain keywords and a brief description of your site.

You should be aware of the three primary meta tags that drive traffic to your site. For example, if you had a dog training website on Jupiter, your meta tags would look something like this:

Title Meta Tag Example

<title>Dog Training Jupiter | Dog Behavior Consultant Jupiter | Dog Professional Jupiter</title>

Keyword Meta Tag Example

<meta name="keywords" content="Dog Training Jupiter, Dog behavior consultant Jupiter, dog professional Jupiter, dogs in Jupiter">

Description Meta Tag Example

<meta name="description" content="Natalie is a certified dog behavior consultant and professional dog trainer who resides on Jupiter and likes to discipline dogs on that large big planet">

An important part of writing a good meta tag is to include keywords that relate to your website. Never spam the meta tag or compress it with lots of random keywords. Also remember to place the most relevant keyword closest to the left side of your tag.

The title meta tag is the most important one to make changes to. If you don't have a good title meta tag for your website, you can figure out what it should be by loading up your website on your favorite browser.

If you don't see a description of your keywords listed in the task bar or the top of your Internet browser when you open up your website, then it's likely your title meta tag hasn't been optimized correctly for the search engines. By simply changing the title meta tag, you can increase your search engine ranking by over 60 percent.

Your keyword meta tag should contain the keywords that are actually written in your website content. If your content contains "I train dogs on Jupiter" then good keywords to include in your meta tag would be "train dogs Jupiter."

Many people believe that simply by putting in a one-word keyword like "dogs" will get them listed high in the search engines. That will never work unless you work with it for over 10 years. The main reason why this doesn't work is that one general keyword you're targeting is likely to be extremely competitive. Examples of this are "money," "dogs," "cars," and "games." You'll never be listed on the front page of the search engines by having that keyword by itself in your keyword meta tag.

However, one way you can get closer to the front page is to break down the main keyword into a niche. They say that "riches are in the niches," and that's true.

A keyword such as "dogs" is too general and large of a market to beat. If you were to target "dog training" then that keyword would still be competitive all over the world. Think about it, over 10 million people type in "dogs" so why should your website be listed first just because you have the keyword "dogs" in the meta tag? However, if you were to target "dog training Jupiter husky" that would give you a stronger chance of dominating the search engines, according to that narrow niche.

What I have just shared with you is a huge secret to my success in getting websites to the top of the searches. You need to "niche down" your keywords and make them more narrowly defined. The narrower your market is, the less competition you'll have, so your chances are better for dominating.

"Niche down" your keywords and narrowly define them.

Having Robots Work for You

Did you know that all successful websites have robots? I don't necessarily mean an actual mechanical robot but a file that acts like one.

There's a file identifiable by search engines by the name "robots.txt." Its function is to tell the search engines which pages to scan for keywords and which to avoid. This file needs to be created and stored on your website server.

For example, for one of my websites that is ranking very well at the moment, the robots.txt file contains the following information:

User-agent:*

Disallow:

What this does is tell the search engines "welcome to my website, you're free to scan the entire website for keywords, would you like a cup of coffee?"

This file needs to be stored in the same location as your home page.

Do You Make These Mistakes in Optimizing Your Site?

I remember the first website design business I started. I was having a nice dinner with my girlfriend. The waiter brought out the drinks menu and on it was a cocktail called "Phoenix Rising." There it was. I saw that name and instantly knew it was time to start my business.

The next day I was very enthusiastic about starting my new adventure, though I knew nothing about business or what was going to happen. I started the business and registered my new domain name. Over the new few days, I found out what I could about search engine optimization. I'm sure you've heard it before, cram as many keywords on your website as you can and watch your website dominate the search engines.

So that's exactly what I did. I wrote the copy then started to put as many keywords as I could into my web pages. I put keywords everywhere. I attached keywords to the title tags, images, and file names. I also put the same keywords on my links and anything else I could tag.

I submitted my domain name to the search engines and waited. I waited for weeks. Several weeks ended up being several months and still nothing happened. I did a few searches for the keywords I was targeting but found that my website never appeared anywhere close to the top.

Frustrated and confused, I decided to do some research to find out what may have happened to my website. After all, it was completely new and should be okay to be listed in the searches, right? Wrong!

What I found out was that I was breaking the search engine rules. I was actually spamming the search engines with keywords and trying to deceive them.

My website was banned and received zero traffic. As a result of this, my domain name was also blacklisted; I had just lost money, time, and energy by building a blacklisted website. My domain name was worthless online and was unprofitable.

I learned the following four lessons from that experience:

Lesson #1: Always write content with the user in mind, not the search engines.

Lesson #2: Never put more than 30 percent of the keywords you're targeting into an article piece. It's safer to sprinkle keywords into your copy.

Lesson #3: Search engines are smart so don't try to outsmart them with fancy techniques.

Lesson #4: Remember lesson #1.

So how do you safely follow search engine guidelines when they're always changing? It's simple.

The Content Writing Formula

Write quality content that focuses on the end user. Don't worry about the keywords you use. When you finish, sprinkle your copy with some of the keywords for your target market and that's it.

That simple content writing formula has helped bring more sales to my client's businesses and bring them up higher in the search engine results. I know it's ironic, but if you don't focus on optimizing and focus totally on the end user, you'll get the optimization results you want.

In a way, it's nice that it's set up this way because at least you know the search engines are working hard to deliver your quality content, not just spam, which makes the Internet a quality environment.

Remember: It's not worth going over the top to optimize your website copy too much, because if you break just one rule, you run the risk of being banned by the search engines. That will result in loosing your domain name and add your marketing expenses.

I predict that the search engines will keep evolving long after this book has been published, and there will be several new ways to increase your search engine positioning, but I believe the search engines will always have the same primary goal. It is this: Always deliver quality, relevant searches for the end user.

If you do this, your website will always be accepted by the search engines and you'll have a greater chance of generating high levels of traffic and sales.

Quick Action Steps

1. Make sure your code is W3C compliant as soon as possible because it's important for producing a high-quality website.

2. Does your site have a proper title meta tag description that contains your most relevant industry-specific keywords? If not, put them there.

3. Place your main keywords into the keyword meta tag area of your site.

4. Ensure your description meta tag has a proper description of what the site is about.

5. Make sure your site has the robots.txt file and that it's stored in the same folder as your home page. You can find examples of robots.txt files online.

Remember and follow the four lessons I've outlined in this chapter.

12

How to Maintain Your Quality Traffic Results

W hat I'm going to share with you now is what I believe is necessary to achieve maximum results from your website. This is where the rubber meets the road. This is where the amateurs are separated from the experts. If you don't apply this one principle, you won't be on the path to online success. This chapter holds everything together.

The Power of Frequency

I remember once I was outside enjoying a cup of coffee. It was a beautiful day. While I was sitting outside drinking my café latte, something happened.

I had an idea. I'd been researching a lot of material on productivity and came across a method called the 3x5 Index Organizer. I applied the principle to my work habits and it improved my time management and productivity. My idea was this: Why not create a quick video, showing how the index organizer works, how it can transform your life, and how to build it?

Keep in mind, it was only an idea and I didn't care too much about the quality of the video. I wanted to get the idea out of my head and "on paper."

I rushed back home, grabbed a piece of paper and pen, drew out a mind map of what I was going to talk about, emptied my 3x5 box, grabbed my digital camera, and started recording.

The night before, I didn't get much sleep, so you could imagine that my eyes were red and I looked tired since it was also the end of a long workday.

However, I started recording and explained how the 3x5 box worked. I explained how you buy the box and index cards at a local office store, then categorize the dividers, etc.

Once I finished recording, I quickly copied the video onto my hard drive and edited it using the free software that came with my computer. The quality wasn't great and the content was average, but I managed to finish the video in under an hour.

I then uploaded that video to my personal blog site. I posted a quick blurb about it and sent an e-mail alert to my list of subscribers. Some people absolutely loved the video and others didn't like it.

A few weeks later, I was at a dinner party and had quite a lot to drink and was driven home. When I got home, I didn't feel like sleeping and thought that I might as well do some work before I went to sleep. I looked around for productivity websites and chose the first one I found, which was Lifehacker.com. Lifehacker is a great community website that promotes productivity and time management. The website also receives several thousand visits per day and a continual flow of new traffic. Even though I was not thinking clearly because it was 1 a.m. and I didn't feel well, I forced myself to e-mail Lifehacker, asking them to feature my video on their website.

About two weeks later, my video was featured on their website where it was seen by hundreds of thousands of visitors. Can you guess what I was trying to achieve with my experiment? Was it to build a great video? Was it to make the perfect product?

Here's a hint: It had nothing to do with the product.

What I was trying to determine was if it's possible to achieve results when you are unwell, unmotivated, and uninspired, or it's not the right time and you haven't gotten enough sleep. My idea was to build something without perfection or waiting for the right time or energy to do it. Every time I worked on this project I did it when it wasn't quite the right time or I didn't have enough energy.

As a result, I became really interested in what happened when I took action, even when I wasn't "ready" and I received a positive result from it. I then drew a diagram of how motivation and action tend to work together to affect your results.

> *Make a habit of doing things whether or not it's the right time or you have the motivation.*

You can see in Figure 12-1 on the next page that motivation directly affects results. Therefore, if you simply form the habit of taking action continually, whether you're motivated or not, you'll get better results in life.

Never wait for the right time, motivation, energy, or passion to do something, because if you do, you'll wait forever. Your ducks will never line up. Just get out there and do it.

The Secrets of Measuring Your Website Traffic

It's important to measure your results. If you're not measuring your results, then how do you know if you've made progress?

Here are some of the major variables you must measure to achieve greater success with your site:

- How many unique visitors you are getting each day? You need to know if you're receiving new visitors each day.
- What are the keywords that are bringing people to your website? For example, are people typing in the right phrases to find you or are they randomly finding you by typing in something else?

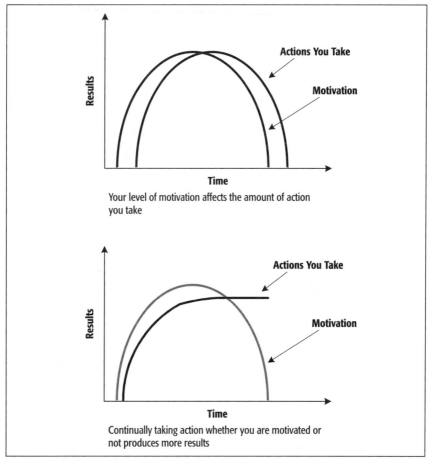

Figure 12-1. The Power of Frequency

- How much traffic are you getting through external links?

One of the best ways to measure your traffic generation results is to use free analytic software like Google Analytics. There are a lot of website analytic software tools out there, but Google Analytics is one of my personal favorites. If you don't already have it installed, I suggest asking your web developer to do it for you.

You've probably been observing the level of your website visitors for a while. Sometimes it goes up and sometimes it goes down. This is the nature of the Internet; it's like the stock market, which depends on current conditions. When you measure your results, you know where you stand, and how and where you can improve. For a start, you probably know approximately how many visitors you're getting per day.

Let's say that you're getting 15 hits per day. Out of those 15 hits, you find that 10 are from people clicking onto your website using someone else's links and the five additional ones come from the search engines. With that knowledge, you know you can improve your efforts for the search engines.

By measuring how much traffic you're receiving, you know whether your efforts are paying off. If you write 10 articles per day and post them on your website, at the end of the week, you'll have 70 articles.

> *By measuring how much traffic you're getting, you know whether you're on track.*

If you knew from your website software which article brought in the most traffic, you'd also learn:

- What your market is mostly looking for
- How hungry that market possibly is
- How you can create a dedicated message to accommodate that small niche market
- Which headline pulls in the best response

For example, I once wrote 10 articles and submitted them to article directories. From that 10, two produced the best results. The other eight didn't produce as much. What I learned was that those two articles had great headlines. The great headlines pulled in a better response than the other eight. Not only that, but the articles I wrote drove targeted traffic to my site.

By studying your website traffic results, you also learn a lot about current conditions. I have a client who was a victim of the horrific Bali Bombings of 2005. He approached me because he was writing a book and wanted to share his heartfelt thoughts and experiences from that tragic event. I immediately began researching the number of people who were searching for this information and targeted his website to those people.

Several weeks later, after launching his website, I noticed that there was a consistent flow of traffic to it and that he was also generating book sales. Several months later, a journalist published a story on the Bali Bombings event and this created a traffic explosion on his website.

By analyzing his traffic results, I could see a spike in traffic due to the story publicized online. From that experience, I learned that:

- New stories drive traffic.
- World events drive traffic.
- A hungry market drives traffic.

If you look at your industry, could there be any event that could trigger a spike in your website traffic? Is your business currently doing anything unique that journalists might find interesting and would want to publish on their media channels?

Another example is tax time. I always found that I would receive nearly double the amount of queries online after July. It occurred to me that most small business owners don't have the funds early in the year to invest in a new website, but when they receive their tax refunds, they have the capital to invest.

I was once studying the number of people who were looking for web design services and noted that the busiest time would be shortly after July. The reason is because the financial year has just ended.

Knowing this, could we not design a marketing package that caters to the financial year? Could we not put together an ad that offers tax incentive discounts to websites? Of course we can!

This all occurs when you test and measure your website traffic and results. But don't fall for the trap of spending more time analyzing your traffic results rather than attracting traffic. Your time should be mostly focused on attracting targeted traffic to your site.

How to Measure Your Website Statistics

Measuring your visitor's movements on your website is without a doubt one of the most important things you can do to bring in more traffic and convert that traffic to customers. The reason why measuring is important is because you won't know where to improve if you don't know your numbers.

For example, let's say that you pay $1,000 to advertise your website on a popular online news website. Then your website receives lots of hits from the news website and you generate three clients from that advertising.

Let's say that each of those clients bought a product from you. That product of yours cost approximately $200. Therefore you made only $600 from that advertisement and lost $400. Should you continue that advertising?

That all depends on if you know your numbers. Let's say that we knew $1,000 worth of advertising caused approximately 100 people to visit your website. Out of that 100, three bought your product. That means your sales conversion rate is 3 percent.

If you knew your website was converting sales at only 3 percent then what could you do to increase that rate? There are many ways to do that. A few examples include:

- Posting a lot of testimonials with results-based stories
- Adding video testimonials
- Adding a strong guarantee
- Adding a strong marketing message with a unique selling proposition
- Packaging your product or content so it appeals more to your target audience
- Selling the benefits of your product rather than the features

What if you knew a lot of people were visiting your website but not taking any action? A great way to figure out why is to have tracking software installed on your website.

Personally, I like to use Google Analytics to track how many visitors I get on my website, where they're visiting from, how long they stay, which keyword they used to find me, and how well I've been doing over the past few weeks.

I once had a website where I received lots of visitors but none of them took any action. I realized that those visitors were clicking off in less than 15 seconds. I figured out that the instant they loaded my website and saw that it wasn't what they were searching for they quickly exited. I then analyzed my own website and discovered a few things:

- It took too long to load.
- It was too cluttered.
- It was hard to find relevant information.

I reorganized my entire website so it loaded properly and displayed easy-to-read information that matched my visitors' interests.

After testing these changes over the course of a few weeks, I noticed that my new visitors stayed on my website for longer than three minutes. That increased the level of business generated by my site.

Why Updating Your Website on a Regular Basis Is Important

Attracting more traffic to your website isn't about doing the work once and forgetting it. I wish I could just create a website, be done with it, and let it continually increase its traffic by itself. Unfortunately this would never happen and hard work really does pay off. If you continually update your website with fresh and relevant information, this is not only a great way for the search engines to index your site, but also lets your users know that your website is continually updated.

If your users know that your website is updated with fresh content on a regular basis they'll continually come back for more and your website traffic will increase.

> *Providing fresh content on your website on a regular basis attracts return visitors.*

I conclude that search engines have a record-keeping system to remember all the actions taken on your website like whether you've been updating it with new information, uploading new products, or using sneaky tactics like spamming or displaying illicit material.

Let's say that you have two similar websites, one that gets updated on a regular basis and the other doesn't. Which website is likely to be more relevant to the searches? Is it the one that has been left alone for many years and hasn't been touched or updated? Or is it the one that's fresh and continually changing with the needs of the users? I'd choose the one that has been frequently updated.

If you want to increase traffic to your website, you must work hard to continually update the site with as much fresh content as possible that's relevant to your industry.

It may seem like hard work to keep coming up with new content for your site, but it really isn't. You can write about anything. You could write about your achievements, give tips, product or service information, or write about any other topic you feel is relevant. Remember it's all about getting visitors to frequent your website. Having many articles on there makes it easier for more people to find you because you've covered a lot of topics.

Giving Something Back

I've found that's it's important to give something free to your users. The reason why it's important is that there are a lot of websites out there that ask you to provide your credit card details or other privileged information. The Internet is a great place to grab a lot of things whether they're free or are paid for. It's always great to give something back to people and if you give something away, and you usually get something in return.

After many years of experimenting with websites, I found that if you have a specific page on which to give away free articles, information, products, or services, it greatly increases the chances of your customers responding to you. It also looks very good to the search engines.

> *Giving away free resources to your visitors increases the value of your website.*

One of the websites I created was for my own web design and development business. When I first created the business, I had lots of ideas on how to present and market myself and how to cater to visitors. I also found that all the other successful websites had a page called "free resources" which contained lots of free articles, links, pictures, documents, spreadsheets, and anything else that may help the user.

If you were a search engine and you came across a website that was relevant to what the user was searching for and also contained a page with free information, would you find this website more attractive, or relevant to your wants, than a page that simply asks for your credit card?

People and Search Engines Love Free Stuff

It's true. Search engines really love free information, especially articles. If your website had lots of helpful articles loaded with keywords that matched what the users were searching for, you would put it in an excellent position to gather lots of free traffic.

We talked about blogs a bit in chapter 4, so you know that a good way to get free website traffic is to write one relating to your industry. By having a blog you can login and create your articles and post them without depending on a web page designer/developer.

You'll notice that when you search topics online there are usually blogs listed in some of the primary search results. The reason why the blogs appear on a high-ranking page is that search engines know they contain lots of information being created on a regular basis and that it's relevant to a particular topic; therefore, blog sites are seen as search engine "friendly."

Free Content Beware

The drawback to providing free information online is that when search engines pick up on the frequent use of the word "free" they may interpret that as spamming.

This also applies to e-mail. You've probably noticed the large amount of e-mail coming through your box that automatically gets dumped into your bulk or junk mail folder. Frequent use of the word "free" is the culprit in a lot of those cases.

Because of the trend in e-mail marketing and unsolicited e-mailing (spamming), legislation has placed restrictive filters on this trend to catch the word "free" in those two venues. Therefore, I highly recommend you not use the word "free" too much in a single article.

A Final Word on Website Traffic

I must say that many people out there have unrealistic expectations when it comes to creating website traffic. Whether you pay for traffic or build it up for free, the whole process takes time.

It usually takes between two and four weeks for your changes to take effect depending on the search engines, if you're taking the free website traffic path. It's a long and steady process. However, if you commit to it, you'll be rewarded for your efforts.

One of the major reasons why you need to be patient with your results is that search engines have all the control. They will always have the upper hand and are continually changing their algorithms to make search results better.

It's easy to give up along the way. After all, who likes to keep on writing, creating content for their website only to see few results the very next day, week, or even month. If that discourages you, then you may need to start testing the paid traffic models as explained in the beginning of this book.

If you were to interview people who are successfully receiving thousands of visitors each month on their website, you'd find that they spent a long time building their content, links, and publicity, until one day it all came rushing in.

I'm the type of person who believes that there are no free lunches in life. It seems as if all the fortunes in the world are hidden away from people who would easily grab them. My point is that if fortunes were easily made, there would be no fortunes left. You have to work at it.

> *The work you put into your website takes time to generate results.*

Let's say that you write up a bunch of articles and submit them to your blog site or article directories. It may take weeks, even months to see your articles generate traffic related to them. I've spent weeks writing up blog articles expecting to generate instant results but that didn't happen. It wasn't until several months later that the work I put into the site started paying off.

One way of learning how to be patient with your results is to not expect instant results. There are many solutions out there that sell the idea of receiving instant traffic for not even lifting a finger. I personally believe that if things were that easy, it would break the universal rules of hard work.

The old adage that hard work pays off is true. There are no short-cuts in life, no matter how fast or easy something appears. If you study successful entrepreneurs, you'll find that they all achieved their dreams with hard work.

One way to break down the hard work is to make it easy to do. For example, let's say that you invest 15 minutes in writing one article per week. By the end of the year you've written 52 articles. Finding 15 minutes is much easier than finding an hour in your schedule. If you look at it at another way, 15 extra minutes per day amounts to 90 hours each year. Imagine what you can do in 90 hours.

Therefore, if you ever feel like you're spending a lot of time on traffic generation and you're not getting those instant results, be patient and keep moving forward. Don't give up!

Quick Action Steps

1. List five things you'd like to have on your website in the next two months that create the most dramatic results. For example, a 12-page report people can sign up to download, a 30-second video of you, video testimonials, etc.

2. Pick an item from your list, schedule a time, and get it done without being perfect.

3. Build the habit of working on projects whether or not you're motivated or inspired.

4. Have an update routine in place to post fresh, new content every month on your site or blog.

5. Brainstorm for free "gifts" you can give to your visitors, like articles, reports, video content, etc.

13

The Cash Website Triangle: The Marketing Side

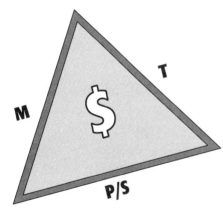

This section of the book is what I consider a hidden bonus. You see, many people think that all they need to do is attract traffic to their site, but really the key is to convert that traffic to sales.

There's no point in setting up your business on a busy street with no signs or indication of what you do. No one will know you exist until you market yourself effectively. So, how do you get those people into your store? This section covers how to let people who may be interested in buying your product or service know who you are.

As explained in the Cash Website Triangle, you need the right marketing to hit the right targeted traffic to succeed online.

How to Convert Your Website Traffic to Sales and the Four Marketing Breakthrough Strategies

There are many ways to convert your traffic to sales. New ways are being invented every day to market your products and services online and offline. However, in this section, I explain the most effective ways to market your products and services online.

The following strategies have worked for me over the years and have proven to be effective in converting traffic to sales.

A lot of people think that once you have a website up and running, all you need is traffic and that's all it takes to make money. Nothing could be further from the truth. The fact is that traffic is not the only important thing used to generate cash with your website. What's more important is converting that traffic.

During the early phases of my web design business, my website was not generating a lot of traffic; it was only getting around seven hits per day, which is not much at all. What I did was look at those seven hits per day as seven opportunities to convert a visit to a customer. Those seven hits were really seven leads, or people raising their hands, saying, "I'm interested."

I began trying a lot of things like optimizing my site, changing a few pages around, updating graphics, etc. A few months later, I was still generating seven hits per day but managed to get one client per month from that seven. Eventually I figured out how to convert all seven hits to sales and ended up with approximately $30,000 worth of new business within a few months, just by tweaking my website.

Even though I wasn't generating a lot of traffic, I found a way to increase my marketing to make the most of the little traffic I had. Many people are in the same situation when they first start a site, dealing with low traffic levels and hardly any marketing strategies at all.

Probably the most surprising fact about this was that I didn't spend any money to achieve that extra income. I simply used my own resources and tweaked and tested all the results I was getting, which led to a positive result.

In the next few sections, I explain how I was able to generate thousands of dollars online with little traffic. I also show you how to apply the same techniques to your website so you can start generating more cash for your business.

Let's get started.

Marketing Breakthrough Strategy #1: Analyzing Results

When my website was generating seven hits per day, I couldn't figure out why people were viewing my website, staying there for a few seconds or minutes, and then exiting. It wasn't until I started analyzing my results and statistics that I found a huge clue about why I wasn't getting any business.

When I opened up my website statistics software, I found the following common pattern with my visitors:

1. Visitor lands on the home page.
2. Visitor clicks on the next closest page, which is My Client Work Portfolio.
3. Visitor leaves my site.
4. Average visiting time is approximately 30 seconds.

What I discovered from looking at my statistics and measuring them was:

- The home page was interesting enough for people to look for more information.
- After they visited my home page, they didn't leave immediately; they wanted more information, so they clicked on my client work page. As a result of this, the home page design was successful in getting them to stay longer and view another page; therefore, no additional work was necessary for my home page.
- After visiting my client work page, they left. This is where the problem was. They didn't fill out the contact form. They just left.

The next step was to analyze my client work page and find out the possible reasons they left. Here's what I discovered:

- My client work page didn't promote my best work up front. It didn't contain enough supportive information for the page.
- The overall design wasn't appealing.
- There was no call to action at the end of that page.
- Overall, the client work page did not promote my services effectively.

As a result of my discoveries, I spent the next few days redesigning my client work page, making it look professional, and more attractive for new visitors.

Making changes to my client work page was a huge breakthrough. About 80 percent of the new people who visited my site and followed the same pattern as before contacted me, inquiring about my business.

People were now not leaving my client work page, rather, they were connecting with me through the contact section at the end of that page, which resulted in new business.

When I discovered the power behind analyzing my results, I was hooked and began to measure everything I did with my website.

Always analyze your website traffic results.

So, what's the best way to measure your site statistics? Use website analytics software. There are many website analytics software packages online that you can search for with the words "website tracking software."

The most popular website analytic software at the moment is Google Analytics. The best part about this tool is that it's free. It also comes with comprehensive measurement tools that are easy to set up. If you don't have a Google account, you can get one by going to Google.com and typing in "google analytics." If the software is too difficult or technical for you to set up, contact your web developer to do it for you.

Rule of thumb: You must have good analytics software on your website and study it carefully.

Marketing Breakthrough Strategy #2: Call to Action

When I succeeded in increasing the number of queries from my website, it really motivated me to try something else. One thing I discovered was that the only page people sent a query from was the contact form page. For example, I only had one contact form and it was on the Contact Us page. That page was the only one they could contact me with. I thought, instead of having a contact form on one page, why not have one on every page? I tested it out and made another breakthrough.

Once again, this increased my queries and resulted in even more business. I believe the reason for this is that, because a person's attention span online is short, they will only use easily accessible information.

My original contact form was hard to locate. A visitor had to go through many pages to reach it. By having my contact form on every page or a link that went to the form, it eliminated the obstacle of having to find the Contact Us link and enabled visitors to easily submit their query.

One great thing about this technique is that it reduces the visitor's urge to close your website. If the contact form is right there, viewers are more likely to take action.

Now before you move on and put a contact form link on every page of your site, I'd like to share another technique for making that contact form more effective. Anyone can put a contact form on every page, but it's the way you word your call-to-action form that makes the difference. Your call-to-action form must be worded in a way that clearly instructs the visitors how to take action.

You must have a strong call to action on your website that's visible and accessible, and contains clear instructions.

Your call to action needs to grab the visitor's attention to either contact you or fill out a form. As a reminder, every website has a unique goal, whether it's to contact your company, download a particular product, sign up for your newsletter, etc. Your call to action depends on whatever your website goal is. Therefore, you need to make sure your call to action relates to your targeted traffic.

Here's an example of a good call-to-action statement that relates to its targeted audience, describes clearly how to contact you, and offers a bonus incentive for doing so:

> To contact us, simply enter your first name, e-mail address, and comments below and we'll send you a free copy of our bestselling e-book *The Seven Ways to Double Your Income in 60 Minutes Without Spending a Fortune,* valued at $29.95. Contact us now.

The wording is important whenever you're writing a call to action. Words are powerful and must be carefully crafted to get the message across quickly and effectively. Also, the call to action font size must be large so it can be easily seen amid your website text.

Here are few ideas to get you started crafting a good call to action:

- Include verbs or "doing" words.
- Offer an incentive for them to contact you, such as a free cup of coffee, initial consultation, or e-book.
- Remove the risk factor for people by including words like "guarantees" or "no obligation" so they don't feel pressured to sign anything. Remember, no one likes to be pressured into doing things.
- Instruct people exactly how to contact you. You'd be surprised how many people struggle to find your contact form or have trouble understanding how to complete it. Remember, it may be easy for you but not for other people.
- Make it easy for people contact you. Don't require them to fill

out a lot of information. A lot of people want to remain anonymous and fear the security risks of sending private information online. If you ask people for too much information, they'll get scared and won't want to fill out your contact form.

- Make it easily accessible. Is it buried under layers and layers of pictures so it's hard to see? Make the form stand out.
- Keep it simple!
- Make your call to action large so it can be seen.

Don't forget to send them to an automatic thank you page after they fill the form out. This builds trust and shows them that you care about them.

Marketing Breakthrough Strategy #3: Massive List of Testimonials

Another great way to increase your sales is to include a massive list of testimonials. This is one of the biggest things you can apply to your website almost immediately.

You may have heard of using testimonials before, and your website may have a few at the moment, but what I'm suggesting is using a massive list of testimonials that overwhelms the visitor with so much proof that they just give up and contact you.

One of the reasons why it's so powerful is that people listen to other people when it comes to buying something. If you have a lot of endorsements as proof that your product or service will help your visitor, you pique their interest.

Build as much trust as possible by loading your website with a massive list of testimonials.

Every time you put a testimonial on your site, the percentage of your respondents will increase. Your job is to collect as many written, photo, and video testimonials as you can.

So how do you get testimonials? It's simple. Ask for them! Don't be afraid to call your clients and ask for them. If you ask, you shall receive.

Marketing Breakthrough Strategy #4: Video

Using video on your website is one of the most powerful ways to persuade someone to buy, sign up for your newsletter, download samples of your product, or fill out your contact form.

The reason why video is such a powerful tool in converting traffic to customers is because people online can't see you. When people can't see who you are, there is a trust barrier you need to overcome. You have to try everything you can to bridge that gap, make it more personal, and help people to see who you are while you're trying to build a relationship with them.

If you have a video of a client raving about you and how great you are, people connect almost instantly to it. They are more likely to watch and listen to what the video has to say than read text.

I'm going to be realistic here. Which one of these would be more likely to grab your attention, a video of a gorgeous person of the opposite sex or pages and pages of boring text? If I saw a video of Miss Universe saying great things about you, it would catch my interest. Then you'd have the opportunity to communicate with me instead of those other people who are displaying blocks of boring copy. Think about it.

> Hi my name is Natalie and I'm the winner of last year's Miss Universe competition. I've been featured in hundreds of magazines and talent shows, and I want to tell you that Bob's product helps me look like a star. You see, I asked Bob to help me prepare for the Miss Universe competition and, as a result of his expertise, I now look incredible and feel confident about myself. He's an easygoing, down-to-earth guy but extremely professional when it comes to personal style. I highly recommend him.

Imagine that video testimonial of Natalie getting viewed not only by the site's regular visitors but also by targeted traffic (people preparing for a beauty competition). If you were preparing for a beauty pageant and saw that video, would you be interested in filling out the form that says "For a free, no-obligation initial consultation valued at $297 that helped Natalie win the Miss Universe Beauty Pageant, fill out the form below." The answer is a resounding *yes*.

Of course, I'm aware that this example is extreme and not everyone can get a celebrity to endorse their business. On the other hand, it definitely doesn't hurt to get 10 video testimonials from various clients saying great things about you.

Videos grab attention, lend credibility, and build trust. You should use videos.

You can do this today. Just pick up the phone, call your current clients, and ask to come by your office to record a quick video for your website. It doesn't cost an arm and a leg, either.

Rule of thumb: Load your website with video testimonials to provide so much proof that people will just give up and take on board whatever it is you have to offer.

Quick Action Steps

1. If you haven't done so already, install Google Analytics or some other website analysis software to measure your website traffic.
2. Spend one hour this month studying your website traffic results and think of ways to improve them.
3. Build a basic spreadsheet that measures the key variables of your website such as: average visitors per day, queries per month, the keywords people are finding you with, how many visitors you get as a result of linking from other sites.
4. Does your website have a strong call to action at the end of every page, like a link to your contact form? Place a strong call to action on every page or at least on the most visited page.

5. Gather a massive collection of testimonials to display on your website. Use a variety of written, photographic, and video testimonials. The "before and after" scenario works well in all of these media.

14

How to Market Your Website for Online Success

W hen you're designing a website, there are a lot of things to consider before that final big step when you connect to the online world. Whether you're building a website yourself or hiring a designer to do it, you must first do some homework.

It's like building a house. First you've got to decide where your ideal location is, how big the house should be: four bedroom, two bathroom, a back and front yard, etc. These stylistic decisions also relate to whether a website will be successful online.

The first question you have to ask yourself is "What's the goal of my website?" Is it to demonstrate your services or products? Is it to get your business on the web so you can showcase it to clients? Do you want to sell products through it? These are some of the questions you should be asking yourself when you're starting to design a website.

Your answers may vary. Asking yourself these questions will help define your expectations, results, and how to build it.

For example, let's say the goal of your website is to showcase your portfolio so people can get a better understanding of what you do. A great design for this website would include more focused information about you, including illuminating your attributes through copy and photos.

The next step is picturing your ideal visitors going to your website. What age group are they in? Are they married, single, corporate, or unemployed? Does their income range between 30K and 40K or more like 100K and 200K?

Once you figure out the goal of your website, you can match its design to suit your target audience. For example, if you've determined you want your website to showcase you and your portfolio and you're trying to target the corporate market, keep in mind that corporate markets are business oriented, have stable incomes, are exposed to a lot of business terminology, and maintain a professional standard.

Once you're armed with solid information, you can design your website. If you want to appeal to the corporate market, you need to design a site that's professional looking and incorporates business elements like photos of people in suits, office environments, and meeting rooms. Your copy should be in professional language rather than slang, informal, or inappropriate phrases that may offend businesspeople.

If you're unsure what a business environment is like and want to appeal to it, you need to research that arena.

Remember, you're not designing a website for yourself; you're designing it for everyone else. Whether your website appeals to your tastes is irrelevant. You're designing for the visitors who are going to be giving you the results you want.

Your target market's opinion of your website comes before yours.

With just a bit of due diligence and homework, your new site will be built on a solid foundation and not on unstable ground.

How to Create the Ultimate Brand Online

Before I explain what constitutes effective website branding, let me ask you what colors you associate with the following brands:

- Google
- Coca-Cola
- McDonald's

Close your eyes for a moment and picture the colors attached to those brands.

What you just pictured in a split second is worth hundreds of millions of dollars. Those companies spend millions of dollars to get you to remember those colors in tandem with their brands.

The reason why branding is so important is because it sets you apart from everyone else. It defines *you*, makes *you* memorable, and sells *you*.

Let's say you build a website that primarily uses the color green. Now let's say you build a product and make it red. If people see your product and go to your website, they'll be slightly confused about you. This also applies to the style and design of your products. Take Apple, for example. Think about how the design and colors of their products are all similar. Yes, their Ipods vary in color but their design is consistent, which holds the look together.

When you spend years building your brand, people come to remember and respect that. Eventually, your brand becomes a quality standard that people will pay a lot for. Your competitors can't steal that from you.

Think of how Bill Gates dresses and the striking consistency of his style. This is no accident. Your style, website brand, and choice in colors are what define you. The Harry Potter books maintain their brand throughout the whole series. How would you be able to quickly recognize them for purchase if they didn't? What if one Harry Potter book had the correct title but a different font, language, writing style, and book cover design? It would confuse you.

If you're just starting out in the business world, it's worth the effort to carefully choose the right color to brand your products and services.

If you brand your website effectively, it'll have its place among the many other companies that spend millions to sit in the minds of others.

Can You Pass the 3-Second Test?

Have you ever heard someone speak about a website like it was a person? I've heard people say things like "The website looks really ugly," "The website is messy," or "The website looks really good!" It's almost as if the website were a human being.

As human beings, we tend to judge things based on what we see. From that, we decide whether something is dangerous or safe to proceed further.

I once read an article that said that within the first 14 seconds of meeting you, people will make assumptions and judge you based on perceived notions of your:

- Age
- Background
- Personality
- Interests
- Behavior

After that, they have mostly made up their minds about you until you change them. The same goes with your website but that doesn't take 14 seconds. It only takes three seconds to be judged.

It takes three seconds for people to judge your website based on their first impressions.

When a visitor glances at your website for the first time, within three seconds they make assumptions based on:

- Your image
- Your relevance to what they're searching for

If it doesn't match what they want, they instantly click off and it's over. If you pass the three-second test, then it takes another minute for them to decide whether your website is ideal for what they really want.

I know that sounds harsh, but it's the truth. I'm sure you've seen websites that took awhile to load just didn't seem to fit what you were looking for and you quickly clicked off.

Because of this, I can't stress enough that your website must be optimized, set up, and targeted correctly for its audience.

On some of the sites I've designed for clients I've embedded tracking software so I could track the number of people visiting and length of their visits. Here are some things I found that make people leave your website within three seconds:

- It takes a long time to load.
- It's too cluttered with information.
- It doesn't match what the visitor is looking for.

Is your site at fault with anything on that list? If so, you're at risk of missing many opportunities online.

Here are a few ways to get visitors to stay on your website longer:

- Optimize your graphics so they don't take long to load.
- Remove unnecessary animation.
- Don't feature music on your website unless it's necessary.

If you feature video clips, make sure viewers don't have to wait several minutes for them to load. They should automatically play as soon as you hit the play button.

How Do You Pass the 3-Second Test?

It's easy; you just need to know which parts of your web page will give you the most effective results.

A recent study analyzed the eye movements of over 500 people viewing websites. The study presented a typical two-column website that contained content and a few pictures. With infrared analysis, they found that viewer's eye movements usually go from left to right and then scan downward.

People usually scan a web page before they decide if they want to read it. What can you do to take advantage of this? It's crucial to place your most important assets near the top of the page and a few going down. If the goal of your website is to have your visitors contact you, place a small contact banner or form near the top of every web page. By doing this, people are highly likely to click on it.

> *People scan web pages first to find information.*

Think about your favorite website. How is the content placed? Is it all copy and no pictures? Or is the content sparse and easy to read? You will find that most news websites use skillful positioning of their images and copy.

Beware of going overboard, cramming tons of information near the top of the page, and expecting great results. You want to have a good balance of space in this location. Don't make it too cluttered. People these days are busy and don't have time to digest a lot of information. Keep this in mind when presenting your site to the audience.

The Power of Attention

I once heard that people hear and see over 3,000 commercials, signs, and ads every single day. If you think about it, with that amount of constant noise and advertising in our faces, it's no wonder we instantly tune out when we sense a sales presentation coming.

If you really want to stand out from all the noise and clutter that your customers see every day, you have to understand the secret of commanding attention.

If your website isn't grabbing the customers' attention, then how can you expect them to take a second glance? By not giving them that "wow" factor, you're just another noise to them.

In a direct-response industry, a lot of people use mail to send out their promotions and sales material. One way they catch the receiver's attention is by using "grabbers" (attention grabbers).

Grabbers can be anything from a ribbon tied around an envelope, a nickel attached to a letter, or a piece of string attached to an envelope and hung on your fence.

Recently a well-known bank sent me a promotional letter. It had a blue kitchen cleaning cloth attached to it. The letter used the cloth as part of its marketing campaign by saying that joining that bank would help clients clean up their financial problems.

How great is that? You see by getting people's attention, it could lead them to take action.

If you had powerful attention-grabbing concepts on your website, like captivating video with *wow* factor, then you're assured your visitor will continue browsing your website and probably take action.

Quick Action Steps

1. List the colors that represent you and your brand.
2. Are your colors consistent through all your online marketing, brochures, reports, and books, etc?
3. E-mail your clients and request their feedback about your site. Ask them their honest opinion of your website at first glance.

15

The Art of Using Emotional Colors on Your Website

My parents owned a busy cafeteria inside an international college. The diversity of students who ate lunch there were from places like Brazil, Japan, Korea, and Switzerland, to name a few.

I remember standing there, watching how everyone interacted with one another. They were mostly laughing and having fun conversations. I noticed they were all in clustered groups of five to eight people.

As I watched, I saw that there wasn't anyone was by him- or herself. They were all alike in their style of clothing, choice of colors, interests, and backgrounds. One group was having a serious conversation, and they all had the same mannerisms. They all had their books and pens out on the table, and lacked designer shoes and cool clothing, but they seem very interested in studying. Another group I watched seemed to all wear similar hairstyles, designer clothes, and handbags. A few of them were putting on make-up.

Every Monday new students would arrive at the school. At first these new students would mingle here and there in different groups, but after a few weeks they would settle permanently in a group of their choosing. It's like they found the wrong group first and then they would finally find the right group and stay with it until they graduated.

What I found is that this is simply the work of nature. We all feel comfortable with something we understand and appreciate. We subconsciously feel more secure when we are with someone who relates to us. I guess this is how not just people, but animals, insects, and sea creatures survive. We all feel more secure when we are part of a group that we understand and appreciate.

If you look at your friends and peers, you'll find that you have a lot of similar interests and values. If you were to go and join another group of people who dislike your interests, how long do you think you could be friends with them? I'm sure many people would answer, "Not long at all."

It seems that we need to be grouped into our circles of people with similar interests to survive. This really boils down to human nature and our animal instincts.

So you might be thinking "How does this story relate to marketing my website?" Well, this chapter is all about colors and how strategically using the right ones can encourage more traffic on your website and convert that traffic to customers.

To do this you need to make your target customers feel like they could join your group comfortably and feel secure about your products and services. You need to make your website as inviting as possible. One way to do this is to make sure your colors match your target customers.

Colors are important to your website's success. They express mood, create an overall impression, and trigger emotional responses. Without color life would be boring.

Although colors are important, don't run out there and color your website like a big gaudy rainbow. You've got to have a strategy.

> *People are emotional creatures, and colors trigger their emotions.*

Colors affect us at a subconscious level. When we see the color red we may automatically think of danger, urgency, and attention. Blue is a calming, trustworthy, and safe color. Are the colors on your website creating the right or wrong impression of you? Do they represent what you're offering and connect with your target audience?

Matching Your Market with the Right Colors

One way to match the right colors to your market is to observe what your target audience is used to seeing. For example, if you were targeting professional and corporate people, what colors might they be exposed to on a regular basis?

When you think of corporate types, what do they wear? Do they wear casual clothes or suits? What colors are their clothes? Take a trip down to the business district of your city to find out.

Once you've done your research you'll notice commonality in the colors that your target audience is exposed to. Once you determine what that color is, you'll want to use it on your site. If the color is blue, for example, you can use a wide range of blues.

Ugly vs. Attractive

Should you design an ugly website or an attractive website? Most people will answer "attractive website"; however, the answer really is, both, and it depends on your market. Over the years I wondered if an attractive website can sell more than an ugly website. I found that they could both sell, depending on whom they are selling to.

If you were looking around online for a designer handbag, would you purchase one from an ugly site? From my experience, people who are interested in designer merchandise want quality and expect it from the beginning of the sale to after the sale has been made.

The service must be of good quality. The website that displays the product must be clean and elegant. The store must be in a prestigious location. The staff must be friendly and fashionable. Everything must be of a high standard with attention to detail.

Remember to focus on what your market is like first and then tailor your message to it. If your market seriously doesn't care about whether your website is professional, then don't present it that way. Present it so it communicates a message the market understands.

How to Get Return Traffic with Effective Colors

When you use effective colors, you're not only relating to your target market, you also benefit by getting a lot of return traffic in the long run. Keep in mind that once your market "accepts" you into their tribe, you gain their trust and they will return to your site.

Rule of thumb: An attractive site that doesn't relate to your target market is not likely to get a return visit. An ugly site that relates to your target market has a better chance to get return visits.

The Secrets of the "Eye Capture" Technique

The "eye capture" technique is important in converting your traffic into sales.

Let me ask you a question. Have you ever been to website and then quickly clicked off? Have you ever wondered why you clicked off the website within three seconds of viewing it?

The main reason people leave a website within three seconds is because it doesn't match their interests. This may be due to poor matching of your message to their desire or lack of design aesthetics or even taking too long to load.

There are many reasons why people don't stay on a website. It's important to understand that, when people visit your website, you've got eight seconds to capture their attention or they'll leave and you'll lose a potential client.

One of my clients had a dull-looking website that also lacked user-friendly design. The average time a visitor stayed on his website was between two and 10 seconds. It was obvious that the visitors were either not interested in the website or something about it prompted them to leave and search for another one.

After having a look at it, I found that my client's key content was hard to locate and didn't match his target market. My goal was to first get the visitors to stay on the site longer.

I applied the eye capture technique to the website and was able to boost the average visitor time from seven seconds to two and a half minutes. This was a huge improvement and his queries and profits both increased as a result.

You're probably wondering what the eye capture technique is. Basically, it's positioning the objects on your website so they follow the usual eye movement when the page is scanned. It's designed to mimic viewing patterns for optimum results.

> *You can attract viewer's eye movements by positioning the objects in the right position on your website.*

Figure 15-1 shows an example of how the eye capture technique works on your website.

After much research I've found that a lot of people view a website from left to right and then scan down the page. This is all done in a few seconds and it's vital to position your most important assets on this common eye movement path.

I like to have only two panels for a basic website. The left panel is the menu and underneath that are testimonials and other important information. The right panel is your main content. On top of both panels is the banner. The banner contains a statement about your services and the title of your site so the user knows where they are.

What usually happens is that a web page will load the top panel first and as that panel loads up the left and right panel will automatically load, as well. It's important to distinguish the left and right pan-

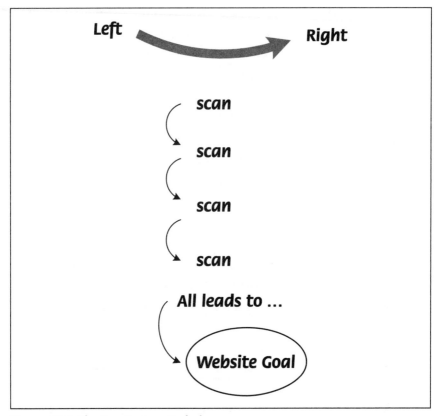

Figure 15-1. The Eye Capture Technique

els. You can do this by applying a stronger color to the main content (right panel) and apply a differing color and contrast to the left panel.

Remember that the left panel contains the menu, and must be highly visible and accessible throughout the entire site.

On the right panel I like to put a large high-quality image to capture the visitors' attention. This is important in keeping them on your website. So if you set up your website correctly they'll see the left menu first, then the right banner with your main eye attention-grabbing image, and then the content displayed under the banner, which is broken up into paragraphs.

Once you set up the website correctly, it follows a common eye movement path. In addition to the good, high-quality image I use in the right panel, I use an image in the top banner to explain what the whole website does. An example of this would be a massage business with a picture of a person getting a massage in the top banner.

For the attention-grabbing image you could display a second image of a person getting a massage to complement what your website is about.

> *Grab viewers' attention by positioning an image representing the end result of your product or service.*

So far we've used two high-quality images in the top banner and the main attention-grabbing right panel. Whenever you use a high-quality image on a website it's going to be slow loading. One way to make your website load faster is to use photo imaging software to optimize the graphics on your website. I recommend using Adobe Photoshop for that, but there are many free options available that also do this.

As you know, if your main attention-grabbing image is large, this slows down your website immensely. Even though many people have higher-speed Internet connections, the search engines in my experience know how long it takes for your website to load on slower connections. If your website loads up fast on a slow connections, it earns points with the search engines.

Consider what would happen if you had two websites. They have the exact same graphics and content. However, one website takes two minutes longer to load on a slower Internet connection. Remember that search engines want to provide the best possible searches for their customers. Which website do you think the search engines would choose as the best search result for its customers? You guessed it, the faster-loading website..

It's pretty important to optimize your graphics and website so they load up faster. This will help you rise up the with search engines and be visible to more people. As a result, increase your traffic and profits if you've marketed yourself effectively.

The eye capture technique is one of the most powerful tools you can use to increase your online sales. A few slight modifications to your website could mean the difference between taking a holiday every three months and one per year.

Quick Action Steps

1. List the colors that your target market is most likely exposed to. For example, corporate professionals would be exposed to blue.
2. Do the colors and images on your website match your target market's preferences?
3. Restructure your website so that it'll grab viewers' attention in three seconds.
4. Follow the eye capture technique by positioning photographs and content that mimic your visitors' eye movements.

16

Using the Grease Slide Technique to Keep Visitors on Your Site

This chapter covers a powerful method called the "grease slide" technique that will enable you to convert your traffic into customers.

The grease slide technique forces your visitors to continually be engaged with your website and stay focused on your copy. Figure 16-1 on the next page illustrates this technique.

The Objective

The objective behind the grease slide technique is to get the visitor to read your copy and become engaged in your call to action. This is an art form and requires a bit of practice and testing to do it right.

Grease Slide Writing Techniques

The grease slide technique is similar to the eye capture technique but applies to only to copy, or text.

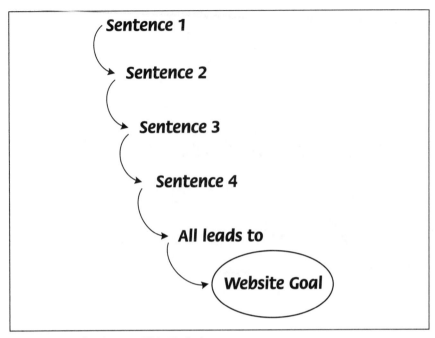

Figure 16-1. The Grease Slide Technique

So, how does it work? When you write words, the way you write is more important than what you write. When you're writing copy for your website it's good to have each paragraph link to another paragraph so it forces the visitor to continue reading.

There are many benefits to this. The main benefit of linking one paragraph to the next is that it forces visitors to engage with your website longer. If you write compelling words, it also encourages trust and coaxes visitors to take action.

An example of the grease slide technique is something like this:

> If you are looking to lose weight then keep reading.
>
> Have you ever tried losing weight and failed miserably?
>
> Have you also tried those diet pills that never seem to work?
>
> If you answered yes to the above questions then you are not alone.
>
> Here's why:

Did you notice the writing style? Have you noticed how each sentence links to the next? This is what the grease slide is all about. It's about getting people to keep reading your content.

Is the content on your website currently linking? Is it boring? Is it too focused on the company and not focused enough on the visitor?

Getting people engaged in your content acts like an approval process for potential customers. Because they've read your content, it proves that they're interested in what you have to say. If they're interested in what you have to say, then they're more likely to be interested in purchasing what you have to offer.

Writing Website Copy That Sells

Writing web copy that sells your products and services is another vital skill you must acquire to generate suitable income from your website. When you write copy for your website, you must first consider to whom you are writing. Whether you're writing to a target audience or a specific individual, you must understand the audience you're writing for.

When you're writing your website copy, write as if you're speaking to one person, not many.

If you're wondering how to write to your target audience, imagine sitting in front an individual, not a mass audience. You'll find that when you write content for an individual sitting right in front of you, your content will be worded differently than if writing for an audience of 1,000 people.

Remember that 99 percent of the time, it's only one person looking at your website and your copy must speak to that one person. Also remember to keep it easy to read and understand. You're writing for clarity, so don't use complex terminology that may confuse the reader.

If you don't feel confident writing your own copy, you can:

- Hire a professional copywriter
- Outsource the work to job markets that contain many enthusiastic writers
- Learn to write it yourself
- Get your web designer to do it for you, but inform them what you want included in the copy

With the first option, if you hire a professional and credible copywriter, your web copy will be as effective as a hiring your own online salesperson. Copywriters are powerful and persuasive people who understand the psychology behind people making purchases online. Some copywriters I know make a killing with their skills because they produce so many sales with their website. However, their skills are not cheap. If you have the cash, a copywriter may be an ideal investment.

The second option is to outsource your web copy work. There are great outsourcing websites such as elance.com and vworker.com loaded with great copywriters. Many people on these websites are willing to take on any online project they can get their hands on.

The websites are secure and have great communication management systems so you can keep track of your work. As a bonus, most people who offer to work with you are affordable and efficient.

The third option would be to learn how to write the content yourself. There are many books out there that teach you how to write your own web copy. You could invest in this specialized knowledge. At the end of the day, it's yours and you can apply it to other projects besides your website, like your own published books.

The final option would be to hand the work over to your web designer/developer. Depending on the situation, and if your web designer/developer has writing skills, it's worth hiring them. However, most designers/developers are focused on their core skills, which is either designing websites or programming them, so make sure you find out if they possess copy writing skills.

Remember that you can also start a blog to practice writing about your thoughts. Eventually practice makes perfect and before you know it, your words will inspire your audience and entice them to take action on your website.

Quick Action Steps

1. Analyze your website content. Does it speak to your visitors or you?
2. Think about the action you want them to take after reading your content. Write your content so it leads them to your call to action.
3. List some problems and frustrations that your target audience is experiencing to build trust and to acknowledge that you understand their situation.
4. Keep your website content simple to read and understand.

17

The Emotionally Charged Website

When I was 15 years old, I was sitting in the library with my class and the librarian was telling all of us that our school now had access to the Internet. Back then I didn't know what the Internet was all about. I remember sitting at the computer with the librarian showing me how to load a website.

One of the first websites I saw was AltaVista. I so clearly remember seeing it. The Web page had a white background and a little copy with a search area and submit button. What really got my attention was the AltaVista logo. The logo included a picture of a mountain.

I did more searches using the AltaVista search engine. Loading up various news websites, I saw more content, pictures, and logos. I enjoyed playing on the Internet because of its visually appealing and creative nature. There were magical icons, clear high-quality pictures of people, and everything was beautifully presented.

I remember grabbing a disk that the librarian gave us and copying all the images from the web page onto it. When I got home from school, I loaded the disk onto my computer and copied all those images from that web page onto my computer.

I looked at all those images and admired them. I loved all the colors, the way the logos were designed, the pictures, and everything else about how they were created. That was when I started learning web design.

A few years later when the Internet started gaining a lot more popularity, more complex websites started popping up. The designs started improving and I became inspired by them.

One of the biggest things I learned about effective web page design had to do with the types of images used. The photographs usually contained pictures of people smiling and having a good time. I found that the websites that got my attention were the ones that had great images.

Invest in good quality images.

The Power Behind Theater

I remember being in New York and wanting to see a popular Broadway show. This show was a best seller and I had to continually approach the ticket booth to book my tickets in advance because for two years, every single day, the show was sold out!

I finally managed to get good tickets, see the show, and enjoy every minute of it. It was a fantastic experience and one I'll never forget. However, there was something I realized. I once heard that if you were to see a high-profile theater production and remove the costumes, set, lighting, music, and leave nothing but the lyrics, you wouldn't even pay two cents for it. Not two cents.

If you don't agree with me, think of a high-profile restaurant that's a whole experience people pay a lot of money for.

Picture this: You walk into a famous restaurant in your city with your partner. A perfectly dressed maître d' formally greets you both and escorts you to your table. As you are being escorted, you notice to your right that there's a man dressed in a full tuxedo playing the piano and singing a beautiful song. There are dressed up couples standing next to the piano, enjoying the music. As you look to your left, you can see the sun setting along the beach through a huge landscape window that's crystal clear. Many people sitting along the window are admiring the view.

As you approach your table, you notice that it has been carefully prepared for your arrival. There are candles already lit, two polished champagne glasses, a white tablecloth with detailed patterns, silver spoons, knives, polished white marble plates, and a small card that says "Reserved" in beautiful handwriting.

Even though I've only described your arrival to this famous restaurant, you can easily picture how it might look.

This is what your website should do; it should create an experience like a high-profile restaurant.

Your website should aim to create an experience for your visitors.

Are you currently creating that great experience for your visitors to your site?

Emotionally Charged, Quality Images

There are many ways to create a better experience on your website. One of my favorite ways is to include high-quality images of people, preferably close-up views of their faces, smiling and carefree. Of course, the images of these people must relate to whatever it is that you're offering. If your website is offering professional services, you would have images of professional people smiling and working.

You can find lots of high-quality images of people on stock photography sites like istockphoto.com or stockexpert.com. These images are excellent at emotionally charging your website and worth investing a small amount in. All you have to do is search for images you want to buy, pay for them, and download them to your computer.

Because it's important to capture the visitors' interests within three seconds, a large, high-quality image at top of your homepage is a good way to quickly connect emotionally. I've applied this technique to many of my client sites and increased their visitors' viewing time by 500 percent.

A word of caution: Be careful not to put too many images on your website because it will slow loading time and your visitors will become frustrated. Also your website may look too busy, and hard to navigate and find information on. I recommend sprinkling your website with high-quality, optimized images.

Emotionally Charged Video

Another way to emotionally charge your website is with video. When you have a video of yourself on your website introducing your business, product, or service, you build a relationship with the visitor. The Internet is a isolating environment and can never replace the experience of speaking to someone face-to-face, but emotionally charged video is the next best thing. You also bridge a big gap between the visitor and you. I've incorporated video into many of my websites and found it to be a powerful tool. It doesn't cost much and is easy to put together.

I once recorded a few video testimonials from my clients. I placed them on my website and a few days later received a business inquiry from a multi-million-dollar mining company. They wanted to meet with me. When I arrived at their office, I met the managers and proceeded with them to the boardroom. The meeting consisted of two top-level managers and me.

As soon as I sat down, one manager said to me, "I've been watching your client videos and see that a lot of people are raving about you." I walked away from that meeting with a $4,500 deal, a $5,000 referral for an upcoming project, and later I was referred for a $10,000 project. By having a video, I was able to bring in just under $20,000.

Later, I realized that the little change in my marketing and video implementation was all I needed to bring in that huge amount of business.

The videos didn't take long to record. They consisted of a couple of minutes of recording time, an hour editing, and 20 minutes to upload to the website. The video promoted my business 24/7 without additional work on my part.

Emotional Copy

Writing for the web is an art form. It's the art of telling your story, demonstrating your product, marketing your services, and getting viewers to take action, which is one of the most important skills to have to run a successful online website.

The home pages of many websites out there say something along the lines of: "Welcome to XYZ Company, we are the best at providing XYZ services, and have been in the business for over X years. We can exceed customer expectations and provide the best service for you."

Does that sound familiar? You may be thinking that it sounds fine, but unfortunately there are two major mistakes in having content written like that.

Emotional Copy Mistake #1

Simply saying "the best" will not do much to get the reader to contact you. If they were to click on one of your competitor's websites, they would get the same message, that that company is also "the best."

Focusing on being "the best" does not differentiate you from anyone else. People will view you as just another XYZ company. Everyone says their own products and services are the best.

Emotional Copy Mistake #2

I'm going to be frank with you: Your readers really don't care about anything you say about yourself. I know that might sound harsh but it's the truth. People tune in for what's referred to as WIIFM, meaning, "What's in it for me?"

If people are reading your website and it's just information about you without any information directed to them, they will become uninterested and disengaged. People come to your website looking for a solution to a problem. If it speaks only about itself and how it's the best company in the world, then the visitor won't relate.

If your website content speaks directly to your viewers, offering solutions to their problems and frustrations, then you'll have their attention.

A Powerful Secret to Converting Your Website Content to Emotional Copy

If you want to seriously turbocharge your website content so that more people will inquire about your products and services, you need to change the way you think about writing.

Writing effective copy is an art form. One way to infuse your copy with emotion is to focus your information on the customer. Instead of talking about yourself, talk about the customer and how you understand their problems and frustrations. Talk about how many people have found your services and products useful.

Make sure your copy is written sincerely. People relate to stories and words that are poured from the heart.

Why Emotion?

Humans are emotional creatures. That's all there is to it.

If you walked into a car dealership, you would see the car sales-people selling the emotion that comes with the car, not the technical specifications. When you think of a convertible, do you think of the kind of metal that the engine was built with, the width of the car, the type of windows it has, or how long the antenna is? Of course not. You're probably imagining a red shiny convertible with the top down and you're sitting in the driver's seat wearing sunglasses. You're cruising through the streets on a sunny day with a smile on your face, getting attention from others.

We purchase things for the emotion and pleasure they give us, not the logic behind them. Remember that we purchase things with 95 percent emotion and justify our purchase with 5 percent logic.

Humans buy things based on emotion and justify with logic.

This is a typical scenario that would be going through a person's mind if they were looking at a convertible at a car dealership.

A person walks into a car dealership and spots a shiny red convertible. While the person is looking at a convertible, they would be thinking about how great it would feel driving it and the attention or status it would confer on them. Of course some people wouldn't buy the red convertible for status but perhaps to make them feel that they're young again, especially for someone experiencing a midlife crisis. We all buy things for different reasons.

While this person is thinking about all the feelings that the convertible will provide, usually the car salesperson says that it's on sale and is available for "easy monthly payments." This person will then be thinking of buying the car because it's on sale and is affordable.

This happens all the time, not just with cars but with clothes, too. It's a beautiful dress, it looks perfect, it makes you feel beautiful, you find out that there is only one left and it's on sale for that day only.

It's important to re-engineer your website marketing so that it's mostly emotionally charged, with just a tiny bit of logic.

Emotional Stories

Stories sell. If you can tell an interesting, entertaining story, from the heart, and relate it to your audience, then I strongly urge you to incorporate it into your website.

If you have stories of your clients' successes with your business, then why not have that on your website? Say a visitor was looking for a financial advisor. He came across your website and read a personal story from one of your clients saying that they were in financial straits, but after working with you, they are now in a much better financial position. This would grab the visitor's attention, wouldn't it? It's better to have a personal story written like that instead of a statement saying that you're the best in the business and provide XYZ services.

A great way to get emotional stories is to e-mail your clients and ask them to provide you with feedback. You could even write the story for them and send it to them for their approval. Obviously they can make changes if they want, and you will have a great story for your website.

Stories don't have to be written. They can be recorded. Why not ask your client out for lunch and bring a tape recorder? Ask them to speak to you about how you helped them, and make the recording friendly and conversational.

If you want to take this even further, you can even take that recording and put it into a DVD product to hand out to prospects and clients. This helps maintain your relationship with your clients and also helps you find new clients.

Quick Action Steps

1. Include stories in your copy to help communicate your message better.
2. Write it in WIIFM (What's in it for me) style.
3. Begin collecting powerful images for your website. Images that display emotion and prompt the visitor to purchase your product or service are perfect.
4. Integrate powerful videos into your website so that they show the end result of using your product or service.
5. Emotionally charge all your website copy so it communicates with the person one-on-one and from the heart.
6. Include stories in your copy to help communicate your message better.

18

The Cash Website Triangle: The Product/Service Side

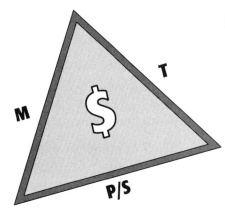

This book has shown you my secrets to attracting a massive amount of traffic to your website. It has also shown you how to convert that traffic to sales with various website marketing tactics. We've finally reached the third part of the Cash Website Triangle that's about products and services (P/S). This segment of the triangle depends on you.

First, if you're reading this chapter, I would like to congratulate you. Ninety percent of people out there don't finish a book they pick up. They will also not apply the strategies outlined in this book. The fact that you read this much means you're dedicated to getting traffic on your site and marketing yourself effectively. Well done!

As outlined in the cash website triangle, the final piece to the puzzle is having a great product or service.

If you're generating tons of traffic on your site and converting that traffic to sales, then it's common sense that your business or company should be providing the right product or service. If you're not doing this, your customers won't return and, even worse, will tell everyone else about you and sully your reputation.

There's no point in doing all this work on your website only to find that your customers don't even find your product useful.

I believe in karma. I'm not saying that you don't provide great service or products to the marketplace. If you didn't, I don't think you would even have picked up this book.

Therefore, this chapter is all about you. It's up to you to provide great service, great products, and great quality. I've met many business owners who are so passionate about their businesses, and there's no doubt in my mind that they're great at what they do.

I know that you're great at what you do, and you're a valuable asset to the marketplace. Well done.

I'd like to conclude by saying that I'm grateful for having this opportunity to share my knowledge and experiences with you. I hope you've picked up a few great ideas and that they'll help you go from sitting on your bike to riding comfortably.

The Cash Website Triangle is an excellent guide to follow as you're building your website. Many of the strategies I've outlined in this book have come from my personal experiences and I've also applied them to my clients with great results.

I hope you'll go out and apply some of the strategies I've outlined in this book. Each chapter has the quick action steps to tackle, so set aside a few minutes each day to take action on your site. Many people tend to read about something but never apply it. You don't need to apply everything you've learned at once. All you need to do is start with one small step.

Just remember, how do you eat an elephant? One bite at a time.

Start this week. Brew a cup of coffee, sit down, block out 15 minutes, and write one article for your website or get that video testimonial. That's it. Do something, just get the ball rolling, and go for it.

Good luck, and I hope to hear from you.

—Khoa Bui

Appendix

The Khoa Bui Website

If you'd like learn more strategies from Khoa Bui, visit his website at **www.khoa-bui.com**, where you can

- Sign up for his free weekly "Online Success Newsletter" filled with secrets for attracting more traffic and sales to your website
- Read Khoa's blog
- Learn about cutting-edge website traffic generation techniques
- Discover the latest online marketing tips and strategies to apply to your site
- Find out more about Khoa's books, DVDs, courses, and other products and services that will help you achieve greater success with your website and business
- Register for workshops and seminars with Khoa Bui

Just visit this site, **www.khoa-bui.com** to learn more about how to dramatically improve traffic and revenue at your website.

Free Gifts to Accompany
How to Increase Your Website Traffic

I hope you enjoyed reading my book. Now I would like to share my complimentary book gifts with you, as a thank you for reading it.

Here's what you get with your complimentary book gifts:

- You'll learn some new ways to increase traffic to your website *not* covered in the book.

- "The Ultimate Traffic Generation Plan" to help you orchestrate your website traffic.

- Become part of the Khoa Bui Gold Member Group and receive the latest news and business strategies

- Receive a variety of tips on marketing your website more effectively that aren't covered in the book. And much more.

If you enjoyed reading this book, then you'll love these free gifts that will help you attract even more traffic to your website and sell more than ever before.

How to Claim Your Free Book Gifts:

Visit the following link, fill out contact information and we'll rush them to you immediately: **www.khoa-bui.com/book**.

Resources

Paid Traffic Resources
Google Adwords, google.com/adwords

Websites for Video Showcasing
YouTube, youtube.com
Revver, revver.com
Viddler, viddler.com
Vimeo, vimeo.com

Article Directories
Ezine Articles, ezinearticles.com

Social Networking Sites
Facebook, facebook.com
Twitter, twitter.com
Myspace, myspace.com

Website Analytic Software
Google Analytics, google.com/analytics

Copywriting Resources
elance, elance.com
vworker, vworker.com

Stock Photography Websites
Istockphoto, istockphoto.com
Stockxpert, stockxpert.com

Create Your Own Blog Sites
Wordpress, wordpress.com

Blog Advertising and Revenue-Generating Products
Google Adsense, google.com/adsense

Keyword Research Tools
Google Keywords, googlekeywordtool.com

Productivity Websites
Lifehacker, lifehacker.com

Index

About the Author

Khoa Bui was born in Vietnam in 1981 when the war was raging between North and South Vietnam. Three months later his family took one of the biggest risks of their lives and fled to Australia by boat. Many boats en route to Australia were attacked by pirates and didn't make it to their destinations. Khoa's family was lucky. They arrived  in Western Australia where they started with nothing and built their new life from scratch.

Khoa started working with computers during the mid 1990s when he learned how to design his own websites. After graduating from Edith Cowan University with a Master's of Science in software engineering in 2003, he began working for various software development companies in education and the private sector as a software developer. Two years later, he followed his dream and started his own web design and development firm, River Designs. Only three years later, Khoa had successfully generated thousands of dollars for his clients through effective website traffic building strategies and Internet marketing.

Khoa co-authored *Counter Attack: Business Strategies for the New Economy* with several American business experts, including celebrity business success and personal development expert Brian Tracy. Khoa excelled over thousands of web design firms and won the TS Design Award 10/10 for Best Design and Development in 2009. He hosted the computer TV series *Byte Me*, featured on the popular "Life Hacker" productivity site. Additional author projects include contributions to EzineArticles Expert Authors series and the National Speakers Association.

Khoa creates online branding, search engine optimization, and design for million-dollar clients in government, mining, education, and the private sector, as well as charities, such as Starlight Children's Foundation and Juvenile Diabetes Research Foundation.

Khoa is a passionate, seasoned global speaker and trainer for events and large corporate staff initiatives. He loves global travel and being an active philanthropist.